Cumbrian Branch Lines: No. 1

The Kendal &
Windermere Railway

The first railway to be built
into the heart of the Lake District.

Dick Smith

**Cumbrian
Railways
Association**

Contents

This book is dedicated to the memory of Harold Bowtell and Alec Mayor, who, each in his own way, added much to the history and enjoyment of Cumbrian Railways

Acknowledgements

The outstanding feature of working on this book has been the generosity of so many people whom I have asked for information. I should like to thank them all, especially:

Jennifer Jewell, a native of Windermere, who contributed particularly to Chapter 4; the staff at Kendal Library, especially in the Local Studies section, and the staff at the County Record Office in Kendal for their help with local archive material; staff at the Public Record Office in Kew; Rock Battye, Gordon Biddle, Alan Johnstone, Michael Peascod, Peter Robinson and Alan Sykes from the CRA for their information and support; Tim Hodgins, who first alerted me to the Kendal Mercury's trenchant reporting; staff at the Library of the National Railway Museum for timetable and accident information; the many former railwaymen, especially Ken Jackson and Tom Moss, who have patiently explained to me some of the special features of working the line; members of the Lakes Line Action Group, especially Robert Talbot, for their help with the recent history of the line; Kendal Town Council and Windermere Parish Council for their encouragement of the project and permission to use items from their records; Mrs D. R. Matthews of G. H. Pattinson Ltd. for providing information from the firm's records; Geoff Brambles for drawing the special map for Chapter 1. My thanks also to Percy Duff for permission to use photographs from the Margaret Duff Collection.

But the help of all these people would have been wasted without the constant encouragement and support of Gill, Kate and Tom.

Front Cover:

The reproduction of the poster is by kind permission of the Science & Society Picture Library. Published in 1910, it promoted the London & North Western Railway as the means of gaining access to Kendal and the Lake District.

The superb heading graphic is the work of Richard Shepherd, to whom the publishers acknowledge their thanks.

**Published by The Cumbrian Railways Association,
a Registered Charity No. 1025436
www.cumbrian-rail.org**

Membership Secretary, 36 Clevelands Avenue, Barrow-in-Furness, Cumbria. LA13 0AE
© The Author and the Cumbrian Railways Association

Design & layout by Michael Peascod,
104 Durley Avenue, Pinner, Middlesex, HA5 1JH
Printed by Lambert Print & Design, Settle, North Yorkshire.

ISBN 0-9540232-0-X

Introduction

IN 1995 the Lakes Line Action Group began to plan celebrations for the 150th anniversary of the completion of the railway to Windermere, and, in preparation for this, I began to look into the line's history. This was the start of a fascinating search through local and national archives as well as the books about railways in the area. It soon became clear that, though the line is just a short branch, the story, especially at the beginning, is complicated and of both local and national relevance.

The first fruits of the search were to be seen in the special leaflet for the anniversary produced by the Action Group and Cumbria County Council, and in the exhibitions which the Group mounted in 1997, one in each of the four communities with a station on the branch. At each of these shows local people who used the line came to look and add their own reminiscences about the branch, which has clearly inspired great affection in its users. Instead of being the end of the celebrations of the line's history these shows became the start of more research. A chance remark about the railway in my day job to an 'A' level General Studies class sparked off a lively discussion, showing the younger generation was interested too, not only in the railway's history but also in its usefulness today.

Finally came encouragement from the CRA to put the story together in book form, using photographs from the Association's archive, and some which have not been published before. I hope that the story I have written shows just how this line, born out of the difficulties of early Victorian steam engines coping with the hill from Kendal to Grayrigg, later prospered, greatly influenced developments in its catchment area and still contributes to its quality of life today.

On a bright winter day in December 1964 passengers wait on platform 2 at Windermere. With its barrows on the platform and empty stock on the central track, Windermere still had the look of a big station.

Photo: Geoffrey Allonby

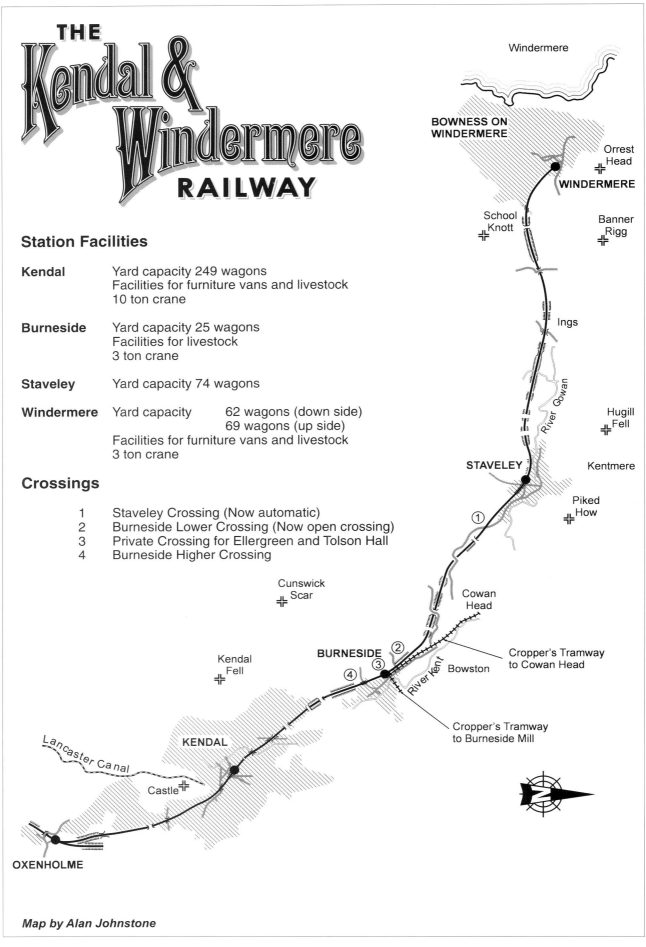

THE Kendal & Windermere RAILWAY

Station Facilities

Kendal   Yard capacity 249 wagons
Facilities for furniture vans and livestock
10 ton crane

Burneside   Yard capacity 25 wagons
Facilities for livestock
3 ton crane

Staveley   Yard capacity 74 wagons

Windermere   Yard capacity   62 wagons (down side)
69 wagons (up side)
Facilities for furniture vans and livestock
3 ton crane

Crossings

1   Staveley Crossing (Now automatic)
2   Burneside Lower Crossing (Now open crossing)
3   Private Crossing for Ellergreen and Tolson Hall
4   Burneside Higher Crossing

Map by Alan Johnstone

1:

Before the Beginning

The machinations which put Kendal on the railway map

WITHOUT a railway Kendal must be thrown into the back settlements. Thus wrote *Observator* to the *Kendal Mercury* in March 1839, expressing dramatically the fears of the civic leaders of Kendal who realised that the plans for a railway from England to Scotland would not involve their town.

They were not driven by simple concerns for prestige, nor merely by the fashion of the time for promoting railways. They could foresee, though perhaps only vaguely, that towns on the railway network would be part of a great modernising and progressive movement, that communication would be speeded up, but also that railways had the solid economic advantage that they reduced the cost of carriage of goods.

Coal was often quoted as an example of what might be. Kendal had few nearby coal mines and imported coal from Wigan at a price of around 23s (£1.15) a ton. Those behind the proposals for a direct rail link to Carlisle estimated that railway transport would reduce this cost by around 6s 6d (32$\frac{1}{2}$p) per ton, a clearly significant saving of more than 25%. Business was not thriving in Kendal at this time and the papers carried regular reports of the problems of the cloth trade and of measures to relieve the distress of the unemployed. This was the time of the slump known as the 'hungry forties', and reports of the campaign for the repeal of the Corn Laws were even more frequent than those about bringing the railway to Kendal. The two campaigns were linked, sometimes by the people involved in them, in that both would relieve the burdens of the poor, who would benefit from cheaper food and coal. These leading citizens were dismayed to find schemes which ignored Kendal being put forward in the race to be the northern section of the railway from London to Glasgow, and they were determined to do something about it.

All the proposals took Lancaster as their starting point. Construction of the Lancaster and Preston Railway was well advanced, continuing the trunk route formed by the North Union Railway, and travel to and from London was already noticeably faster. The *Mercury* reported in September 1838 that *from Monday next, the London mails, via Birmingham, will reach Kendal by 3 o'clock in the afternoon of each day. The railway system is, indeed, destined to work a revolution in our means of locomotion.*

From Lancaster the most direct route was planned to follow the Lune valley, taking it through Kirkby Lonsdale and the Lune Gorge. This line would avoid the worst of the natural obstacles until it reached Shap, where a tunnel - over a mile in length in the first surveys, later reduced to 880 yards - would avoid the highest part of the fell before the line headed down the valley towards Penrith. The maximum gradient would be 1 in 100, which Joseph Locke, the engineer charged in 1835 with surveying routes northward to Carlisle, felt was perfectly reasonable to be tackled by the locomotives of the time.

The alternative proposal, which had the advantage of being recommended by no less a person than George Stephenson, avoided the stiff climb and the wild country of the Westmorland moors by following the coast. It was longer, around 96 miles to Carlisle as against 67 via Shap, but, as its proposers pointed out, it would pass through the well populated West Cumberland towns of Whitehaven, Workington and Maryport with their rich coal and iron reserves. Furthermore the proposers could promise an economic miracle, a railway line that would cost nothing to build and so guarantee a healthy profit to its backers. This favourable start would come from the way the line would cross Morecambe Bay, where the proposal was for an embankment which would create hundreds of acres of fertile farmland which could be let or sold. John Hague, a civil engineer, resurveyed the route across the Bay in 1838 and *not a doubt now exists as to the practicability of an embankment being made.* The *Whitehaven Herald* reported that its glowing prospects included *surplus revenue of at least £100,000 per annum* and, in September 1839, specimens of grass were put on display in Ulverston to show how fertile the reclaimed lands would be.

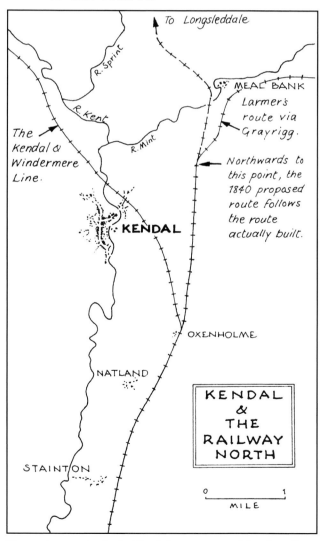

The various routes in the Kendal area proposed for the railway to Scotland. **Drawing by Geoff Brambles**

Such a bold scheme was competition indeed for a line over the fells, and the *Kendal Mercury* and some of its readers clearly felt threatened enough to have to ridicule the proposal. A correspondent calculated that, assuming the embankment would have to be 7 yards high in order to hold back a 20ft. tide, then 677,600,000 cubic yards of soil would be needed to create the 20,000 acres of farmland promised in Stephenson's survey; Hague expected to reclaim at least 46,300 acres. The *Mercury* itself attacked the engineer's report, saying it did *not appear to be a business-like paper,* contrasting it unfavourably with *the doings of the originators of the Penrith and Carlisle Railway,* the foremost scheme for a direct route at the time, and, of course, one which held out the prospect of the railway coming through Kendal. *Civis* wrote to point out that the Morecambe Bay line would close Milnthorpe as a port and recommended the Kent be embanked to allow coal to be shipped direct to Levens Bridge for onward transport to Kendal; this would reduce the price in Kendal by 4d or 5d a hundredweight.

Eventually the Government appointed two Commissioners, Sir Frederic Smith RE, and Professor P W Barlow to look into the question of a railway from London to Scotland, and backers of the various schemes submitted their proposals for consideration. In its first edition of 1840 the *Mercury* did its best to upset the Bay scheme by accusing the coast line party of submitting false information - they had apparently inflated the figure for the population their line would serve and given the wrong figure for the length of the line.

There was a third proposal which had been considered by Locke and was sufficiently advanced to be submitted to the Commissioners in January 1840. This was for a line from Lancaster to Kendal, along the valley of the River Sprint up Longsleddale where it would tunnel under Gatescarth Pass to Mardale, and then along Haweswater to Penrith. As far as its promoters were concerned this scheme answered all possible criticisms. It passed through Kendal, promised mineral wealth in Mardale, had easy gradients with a maximum of 1 in 144 and shortened the distance to Carlisle. This line really was Kendal's proposal, with a committee led by Cornelius Nicholson backing it, even going so far as to commission a proper survey by the local surveyor Job Bintley and Lieutenant Fanshawe, who undertook the prospecting for Gatescarth Tunnel. Prudently they had been to see Joseph Locke, surveyor of the Lancaster and Preston Railway, to obtain his support for their line, which would start from the L&P terminus.

KENDAL & WINDERMERE RAILWAY

AT A SPECIAL MEETING of the PROPRIE-
TORS of this Undertaking, held at the Com-
MERCIAL INN, in Kendal, on Tuesday, 5th day of No-
vember, 1844,

EDWARD WILSON, Esq. F.G.S., of Abbot Hall,
in the Chair,

It was moved by the CHAIRMAN, seconded by JAMES
BRYANS, Esq., Bellfield, Bowness, and

Resolved, I. That it is the opinion of this Meeting, in conformity with the recommendation of Mr ERRINGTON, the Engineer, that the Northern Terminus of the Line should, and the same is hereby ordered, to be at Bir-thwaite, near Bowness.

It was moved by CORNELIUS NICHOLSON, Esq., of Cowan Head, seconded by JOHN HARRISON, Esq., of Hundhow, and

Resolved, II. That the Thanks of this Company be given to JOSEPH LOCKE, Esq., F.R.S., the eminent En-gineer, for his conduct in the preliminary measures of the Undertaking.

Mr Wilson having left the Chair—

It was moved by HORNBY ROUGHSEDGE, Esq., of Fox Ghyll, near Ambleside, seconded by JOHN DAVY, Esq. M.D., F.R.S., and

Resolved, III. That the cordial Thanks of this Meet-ing be presented to EDWARD WILSON, Esquire, for his conduct in the Chair and general services to the interests of the Company.

Public notices put in the Kendal Mercury *by supporters and opponents of the line. The printer has used the same railway block for the opposing notices.*

KENDAL & WINDERMERE RAILWAY

AT a MEETING of the Owners of Lands in the Neighbourhood of Ambleside and Bowness, through which the proposed Railway would pass, and of others, whose Interests may be affected thereby, held at the LOW WOOD INN, on WEDNESDAY, the 2nd of OCTOBER, 1844,

PROFESSOR WILSON, in the Chair,

Various Resolutions were carried unanimously, and amongst others the following, that the proposed Railway should be opposed, and that a Committee should be ap-pointed to conduct such opposition,—that the following Gentlemen should be appointed the Committee, and they were appointed accordingly, viz.—Thomas Jackson, Esq.; Thomas Benson, Esquire; George Partridge, Esquire; Mr Edward Garnett; George Law Newton, Esquire; Jas. Pennington, Esquire; Benson Harrison, Esquire; Cap-tain H. T. Lutwidge; Mr Nicholas Wilson; Mr William Birkett; Mr Ullock; and The Reverend Dr. William Pearson, with power to add to their numbers. A Sub scription was immediately entered into for defraying the Expenses of conducting the Opposition.

The following Individuals have since been added to the Committee, viz.:—

THE EARL OF BRADFORD.
PROFESSOR WILSON.
WILLIAM WORDSWORTH, Rydal Mount, Esq.
THOMAS DAWSON, Allan Bank, Esq.
RICHARD LUTHER WATSON, Calgarth. Esq.
HENRY CHRISTIAN CURWEN, Belle Isle, Esq.
The Rev. FLETCHER FLEMING, of Rayrigg.
The Rev. JOHN DAWES, of Ambleside.
CHARLES PARKER, of Park Nook, Esq.
BENJAMIN HOPKINSON, of Ambleside, Esq.
RALPH ALCOCK, of Grasmere, Esq.

R. & R. MOSER, Solicitors.

Cornelius Nicholson, moving spirit behind the plans for the K&W and Mayor of Kendal at its opening. This portrait hangs in the Council Chamber of Kendal Town Hall.
Courtesy Kendal Town Council

According to the *Mercury* the deputation from the Kendal Committee *received the highest encouragement from Mr Locke.* The scheme included plans for an engine works in Kendal, which caused some local opposition from those who did not want to see the town become an industrial centre. When the Commission turned the scheme down, the LNWR (which had a large financial interest in the proposed Lancaster & Carlisle Railway) used the plans as the basis for its own Crewe Works. Had the line been built it would surely have ranked as one of the most spectacular routes in the country as it passed through the impressive ruggedness of Longsleddale before emerging into the more open beauty of Mardale and Haweswater.

If, however, we look into it in detail we can see that it had one flaw, since it did not actually pass through Kendal town, which at that time was situated almost entirely on the west bank of the Kent along Kirkland, Highgate and Stricklandgate. Its route would have gone *by Stainton, east of Natland, to Oxenholme and Larch Hill, leaving Kendal about 1 mile to the west, and .... along the high ground to Meal Bank.* At this point it would have crossed the River Mint. Thus, as the map on page 5 shows, it would not have approached nearer the town centre than the eventual plan for the Lancaster and Carlisle with its station at Oxenholme, a feature which became a growing concern to the people of Kendal.

The Commission worked quickly, but this must have been a nervous time for the backers of railways as it was expected that only one route to Scotland would be recommended, thus dashing the hopes of either the east or the west side of England. As regards the west side of the country, reports in the *Carlisle Journal* in March suggested the Commission favoured the line through Westmorland, whereas the *Lancaster Guardian* was sure the Commissioners had been impressed by the Bay line during their visit to the city.

Finally, in June, the *Mercury* could report triumphantly that *the 'Mariners' must feel bitter disappointment* as the Commissioners pronounced in favour of a western line and opted for the direct route north. The Kendal Committee must, even so, have had mixed feelings, for the Commissioners had effectively killed off their Longsleddale proposal by calling it *difficult*, and had preferred the Lune valley line. They must have been relieved to find, when they read the whole report closely, that all was not lost. The Commissioners, aware that without adequate custom no line could survive, realised the potential business offered by Kendal and noted: *if a line has been found which would afford the advantage of direct railway communication to Kendal ...it might be more beneficial to the Lune line.* Spurred on by this sentiment the members of the Kendal Committee set about finding a way of bringing the Lancaster and Carlisle to Kendal without losing the advantage of the shorter route north over Shap.

They commissioned George Larmer, who had already done some work on the various earlier surveys, to look again at the possible routes north, and in July 1840 he proposed a route which would bring the line nearer to Kendal before continuing north via Grayrigg to join the Lune valley route he had himself proposed to the Commission. Kendal's station would be between *the turnpike from Kendal to Sedbergh and the public roads by Birklands.* In effect he took the southern section of the Longsleddale route and then turned east towards the Lune, but there were two drawbacks: it was two miles longer than the Lune valley route, and included another steep incline from the Kent valley towards the Lune. On the other hand, the landowners along the Kendal route were generally in favour of it, whereas there was opposition in the Lune valley. Lt. Colonel Smith, Parliamentary Commissioner, looked into the question and in due course recommended the *adoption of the Kendal line, though two miles longer, for the sake of Kendal.*

If the absence of railway news in newspaper columns tells a true story, action to promote the railway slackened off after this decision and some readers obviously feared complacency had set in. In April 1841 the Great North of England Railway opened, and the *Mercury*, fearful that commercial success on the East Coast might persuade promoters of the western route to stop at Lancaster, urged *let the Kendal Committee reorganise itself* and carry the Lancaster and Carlisle project forward. Indeed the threat to Kendal was not over and, as late as February 1843, another danger appeared. The Lancaster Canal Company resolved to offer £50,000 to the 'Caledonian Railway' (they meant the L&C, but the term 'Caledonian' was often used to mean any railway to Scotland) *on condition that the line should pass up the Lune and omit Kendal.* The *Mercury* pulled out all the stops with its editorial riposte: *Will Kendal submit to be beggared by a mere knot of men, who have avowed, and are acting upon, the very worst and vilest principles of mercenary selfishness and monopoly?* A week later it was still whipping up opposition to the Canal Company, declaring that if the company succeeded *Kendal will shortly be ranked among the ruined and decaying boroughs of England.* For once there was no difference of opinion between the *Mercury* and its rival, the *Westmorland Gazette.* When news of the Canal Company proposal broke the *Gazette* thundered: *Of all the attempts which we have seen to hoodwink Parliament and cheat the public, this is certainly the most gross and iniquitous.* Faced with determined opposition, the Canal Company backed down in March after persuading the L&C to guarantee the Canal an income of at least £11,000 annually.

WINDERMERE RAILWAY STATION HOTEL

An early view of Kendal & Windermere station at Birthwaite. The station stands in splendid isolation, with only the railway hotel nearby. Other buildings soon sprang up nearby as Birthwaite became transformed into Windermere village.
Courtesy Cumbria County Libraries

As the danger of routes to Scotland that did not include Kendal diminished, the people of the town had time to consider what kind of a railway they had been offered. Despite the influence of such prominent Kendal citizens as Cornelius Nicholson and John Wakefield, the route which the Lancaster and Carlisle Railway settled on did not really come to Kendal. Like the earlier Longsleddale proposal, it would approach no nearer than Oxenholme, and for the very same reason: the engineer did not want to lose height by bringing the line down into the town, only to have to climb back again in order to cross the next range of hills. Avoidance of unnecessary gradients had been the reason for many of the conflicting plans for the line to Scotland, and since the adoption of the Oxenholme

and Grayrigg route added hills which the original Lune Valley proposals had avoided, Larmer was not keen to lengthen these climbs.

The men of Kendal who had been active on the Kendal Committee of the Lancaster and Carlisle realised that only by promoting a separate line which would link Kendal with the trunk route could they realise their ambition of bringing the railway to the town. In August 1844 the two rival papers again spoke with one voice as the *Mercury* reported with satisfaction that it had seen a proposal for a railway from Kendal to Windermere, connecting with the Lancaster and Carlisle at Oxenholme, a scheme which the *Gazette* welcomed, saying *to Kendal, the capital of the Lake District, the line offers manifest advantages.*

2:

The Kendal & Windermere Railway

The plans become a reality

Ex-LNWR 4-4-2 **Precursor** *tank No. 6782 approaches Plantation Bridge with an up train in LMS days. The extra height signal post on the down line permitted early sighting of the signal on the approach to Staveley Crossing.*
Photo: H. Gordon Tidey/NRM Collection. Ref. T8343.

THE list of the provisional committee of the proposed Kendal and Windermere Railway, included in the public notices in August 1844, contained many of the prominent families in the area. At the top of the list were Edward Wilson of Abbott Hall, John Wakefield of Sedgwick House, and G B Crewdson of Kendal. These men represented three of Kendal's foremost families who in a previous generation had taken part in another social revolution when they founded the first banks in Kendal. These were men of some importance. The Wakefield family is still actively involved in Cumbrian railways, as the family company, Lake District Estates, owns the Ravenglass and Eskdale Railway.

Cornelius Nicholson of Cowan Head, who as Interim Secretary had published the notice, was a man with quite a different background. He was born in 1804 in Ambleside where his mother was Postmistress, and, as his father died while Cornelius was still young, he could not have the intended education he longed for. At the age of 14 Nicholson moved to Kendal to learn a trade - printing. He clearly learned quickly, as by 1825 he had a partnership in the bookselling and printing firm of Hudson & Nicholson, and he was also making a mark for himself in civic life and catching up on his missed education. He was one of the founders of the Kendal Natural History and Scientific Society, and in 1832 he published a lengthy history of his adopted town, *The Annals of Kendal*. The same year he started manufacturing paper at Burneside, helped by capital

borrowed from John Wakefield, and in 1837 he published a call to arms, or rather to rails. His pamphlet 'The London and Glasgow Railway: the interests of Kendal considered' set out fears for what would become of Kendal without a railway and hopes for the advantages which a railway would bring to the town and its people. It would, apart from lowering the cost of raw materials, *annihilate space and time* and thus open up distant markets to Kendal's manufacturers. He expected the Kendalians to benefit from cheaper, imported foodstuffs: *At present, Kendal is ill supplied with sea-fish. What we do get is tainted before it arrives here … But with railway communication we should have fish of all kinds, for the poor as well as the rich, fresh and at a moderate price.*

Nicholson, a director of the L&C until 1846, was well aware of the attractions of his native region and claimed that the railway would enable *the merchant princes of Liverpool, and the cotton lords of Manchester, to exchange in a few hours the smoke of their factories and the 'miasmata' of their home towns for the salubrious airs and the silvery mists that floated round the hills.* Probably not even Nicholson realised just how much he would be proved right in this hope, as the better-off merchants of Manchester did indeed use the railway to enable them to have their home at Windermere, as a later chapter shows.

The less well-off were not forgotten. Though Nicholson did not expect them to come and live in the Lake District, he was sure there would be benefits to their physical and spiritual health. He hoped the line would be *signally useful to the working classes in drawing them away from the haunts of vice and intemperance, and opening out to them the beauties of nature by which their minds would be enlarged and hearts expanded.*

The route that these gentlemen proposed saw the railway descend on a long curve from Oxenholme towards Kendal, where there would be a station on the north-eastern edge of the town near where the main road north (now the A6) left the town. The line would then follow the valley of the Kent through the villages of Burneside and Staveley, where it would swing westwards over Banner Rigg towards Windermere. From the hamlet of Birthwaite, high above the lake and 1½ miles north-east of the ancient village of Bowness, the line would move close to the eastern shore of Windermere, running northwards to a terminus at Low Wood, near Ambleside.

Not everyone in the area was in favour, and on 2nd October 1844 a group met at the Low Wood Hotel and set up an opposition committee under Professor Wilson. By 19th October the Committee had been enlarged and added four extremely powerful names to its list: the Earl of Bradford, Mr H C Curwen of Belle Isle, Revd F Fleming of Rayrigg and Mr W Wordsworth of Rydal. Mr Wordsworth expressed his opposition in a sonnet published on 26th October:

Is then no nook of English ground secure
From rash assault? Schemes of retirement sown
In youth, and 'mid the busy world kept pure
As when their earliest flowers of hope were blown,
Must perish; - how can they this blight endure?
And must he too the ruthless change bemoan
Who scorns a false utilitarian lure
'Mid his paternal fields at random thrown?
Baffle the threat, bright Scene, from Orrest-head
Given to the pausing traveller's rapturous glance:
Plead for thy peace, thou beautiful romance
Of nature; and, if human hearts be dead,
Speak, passing winds; ye torrents with your strong
And constant voice, protest against the wrong.

Many of those in the opposition group were, not surprisingly, landowners whose land would be taken by the railway, and who thus stood to lose some privacy.

Wordsworth, living at Rydal, would not have been personally affected but his opposition was no less sincere. He was worried about the loss of tranquillity which the influx of uneducated visitors would bring, and he wrote to the *Morning Post*: *Good is not to be obtained by transferring at once uneducated persons in large bodies to particular spots.* There must be *a great disturbance of the retirement and in many places a destruction of the beauty of the country.* Sadly for Wordsworth, his was largely a lone voice, for the promoters of the Kendal and Windermere Railway soon dealt with most of the opposition by simply redrawing the map and having their line finish at Birthwaite, sparing the land of most of Prof. Wilson's committee members. Mr Errington, the engineer for the line, had in any case recommended terminating the line at Birthwaite in order to save the expense of the heavy works needed on this most northerly stretch of the line, which was a further reason for abandoning it.

Wordsworth was left isolated and tried to use his position to influence people in authority. Two local MPs, Colonel Lowther and Alderman Thompson, had agreed to pilot the Bill through the Commons; Lord Brougham would look after it in the Lords. For his part Wordsworth wrote to Gladstone urging him to object to the bill, because *the project, if carried into effect, will destroy the staple of the country which is its beauty, and on the Lord's Day particularly, will prove subversive of its quiet, and be highly injurious to its morals.*

Such impassioned opposition was perhaps surprising. Some years earlier Wordsworth had written to his wife, *I like railway travelling very much,* and he had himself given tourism in the Lake District a great boost with the publication in 1810 of his own *Guide to the Lakes,* which was reprinted regularly until 1835. The railway, however, threatened to bring such large numbers of visitors that Wordsworth could not imagine how they could be absorbed without damaging the beauty they had come to see. In December 1844 he wrote in his letter to the *Morning Post*: *Look at the little town of Bowness, in the event of such railway inundations. What would become of it in this, not the Retreat but the advance of Ten Thousand.* He believed that it took education to appreciate properly the beauty of the District and that the *cheap trippers* brought in by the railway would fail to appreciate it correctly.

The wool warehouse, built by John Whitwell, a director of the K&W. It had its own siding from the goods yard across the road. It is now the Kendal Museum, housing the archives of the Kendal Natural History and Scientific Society, itself founded by Cornelius Nicholson.
Photo: Margaret Duff Collection

*A pair of **Patriot** class engines brings up a heavy train off the branch and onto the main line at Oxenholme. The 1 in 80 climb from Kendal was a severe test for the locomotives, especially with a long train such as this.*

Photo: CRA Bowtell Collection

Though they printed Wordsworth's objections, the Kendal papers continued to support the railway. On 26th October 1844 the *Mercury* published the now-famous sonnet, but expressed itself clearly in the editorial: *The town of Kendal is vitally interested. If we do not, by means of the Windermere railway, secure to ourselves the passage of the traffic into the [Lake] District, it will pass by us. Milnthorpe and Winster, and Ulverston and Fleetwood will take the lead and Kendal will become one of those 'nooks' with which Wordsworth is so much enraptured.*

Wordsworth's intervention certainly caused a stir (and so perhaps helped the railway by giving it more publicity). On 9th November the *Mercury* printed no fewer than three sonnets, all in opposition to the anti-railway point of view. Two were written as direct ripostes, one appearing in the *Scotsman*, one in the *Glasgow Citizen*, but the third, embarrassingly, was by Wordsworth himself – an earlier work in praise of *Steamboats and Railways*.

Despite all his influence and stature Wordsworth's protests came to nought. He was trying to swim against the tide and for every one of his objections there were more counter-arguments - even the moral arguments - on the side of the promoters. Those who objected to the railway were seen as anti-progressive and snobbish. Almost a year after the first objections, the *Mercury* printed a wonderful notice from *Miss Ann Thrope* and others in which the elitist objections to the railway were lampooned. The railway should be stopped because: *it would make coal cheap, and break down the distinction between the fires of the rich and poor. We like the smell of peat and like to see the small column of blue smoke rising from an occasional cottage. But railroad prices will raise a cloud of black coal smoke from every house alike, which is horrible to think of. Blazing fires were never intended for poor people.* And, in perhaps a conscious echo of Wordworth's objections: *it will bring crowds of vulgar people to jostle against us and disturb our charm of solitude.*

In its editorial of 24th August 1844 the *Mercury* had welcomed *this well-conceived and timely project.* It praised the landowners who had *signified their assent* to the scheme and had asked to be shareholders not for personal gain but *with the view of assisting to promote what cannot fail to be a most laudable, useful and beneficial work.* With its backers displaying such altruism, the railway was bound to be a success. On a practical level, the *Mercury* pointed out that the scheme would *give the town of Kendal the advantage of a proximate station*, which neither the Lancaster and Carlisle nor the earlier Kendal proposal for a line up Longsleddale would have done. The share offer was so popular that subscriptions were closed on 14th September, earlier than expected, and on 28th September the shares were reported as trading at a premium of 15 to 20 shillings.

The Bill was presented in Parliament, received the Royal Assent on 30th June, and construction began. Cornelius Nicholson cut the first sod on 16th July in front of *a considerable concourse of spectators.*

Joseph Locke, the supervising engineer for the L&C, was appointed supervisor for the K&W, with John Harrison as his assistant. The actual construction was undertaken by Thomas Brassey and John Stephenson & Co., and was under way within a couple of weeks of the Royal Assent. By this time the original proposal for a single line railway had been upgraded to double track, but as the engineers met few problems in their work, the overall cost remained within the original budget.

The promoters had been so confident of success in Parliament that they let the contract with Stephenson & Co. in March, three months before the Royal Assent. Any doubts about the wisdom of this move must have been reduced when, in April 1845, the Board of Trade's Railway Department reported favourably on the proposal, saying *we are of the opinion that there are no public grounds which ought to be decisive against the K&W … receiving the sanction of Parliament.*

Burneside station in LNWR days. The platforms were offset, and the road to Tolson Hall crosses the line between them. The station house still stands, though in private ownership. The crossover led into the goods yard.

Photo: Cumbrian Railways Association Collection

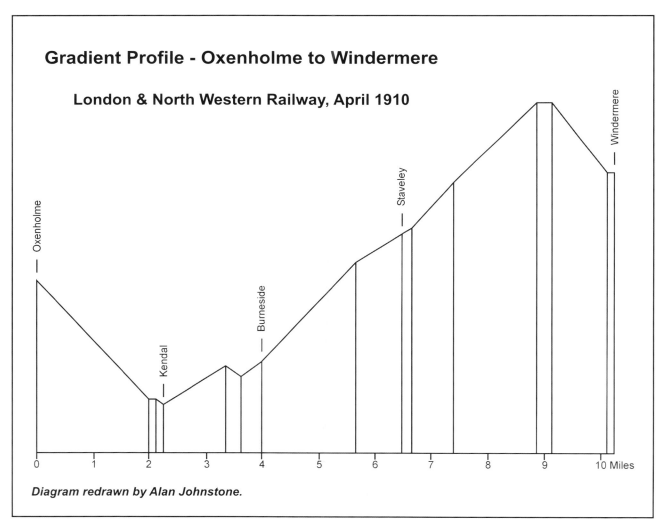

Gradient Profile - Oxenholme to Windermere

London & North Western Railway, April 1910

Diagram redrawn by Alan Johnstone.

The tide was running in favour of railways, and at this time many proposals were made which never came close to realisation. Among these was the 'Furness and Windermere Railway' which would have run along the east side of Windermere, linking with the Furness Railway at its southern end and with the K&W at its northern. The front page of the *Mercury* of 15th November 1845 was composed entirely of railway notices, for six companies in all. However, by May 1846 the directors of the proposed F & W had decided not to go north of Newby Bridge, leaving the K&W as a *mere offshoot*, as the K&W had called it earlier when supporting the F&W proposal.

The actual construction of the railway went well. In the autumn of 1845 there were moves to bring the Kendal station nearer the town centre, but these would have involved building a short extension, rather than altering the route as a whole, and were not successful even though Cornelius Nicholson seemed to be in favour at one time. On 1st November the *Mercury* reported that *Constable Furness of the Kendal police* had been appointed on the Windermere line. He was either very efficient or the workforce well-behaved, for there are very few references in the papers to trouble on the K&W, in contrast to the L&C where accidents and violence seemed quite common. The only major incident was in February 1846 when some masons from the K&W joined English and Irish masons from the L&C in a riot near Penrith, but the magistrates *took prompt measures for preserving the peace* (they called out the yeomanry cavalry) *and all incipient disturbance was quickly crushed* without the need to use the special constables who had been sworn in. In another case a local took the law into his own hands. He was a shopkeeper in Staveley, who had supplied one of the navvies with food to the value of 17 shillings, to be paid for on pay night. The shopkeeper made sure he was close by when the navvy was paid, but the debtor ran off. The *Mercury* reported:

The man of groceries instantly trimmed sail, and away he went in pursuit, with the fleetness of a greyhound. The navvy set off towards Ambleside, but turned off for Bowness, where he took the Crook road and *after a chase of more than two hours duration, finding he could not evade his relentless pursuer, he again made for Staveley, where he 'earthed' in a cesspool.* The shopkeeper hurled stones at the navvy, who eventually gave in and paid up, then slunk away to hide *from the hearty jeering of his companions.*

There were some accidents during construction. On 20th June 1846 the *Mercury* reported William Kettle had been thrown onto his head when the team of wagons he was driving ran away. The most difficult part of the work was cutting through slate near Staveley. This required blasting, and in November 1846 Edward Houston was injured in both eyes as a charge went off late, just as he was investigating it. Two days earlier a fellow worker had been hurt by flying rock. A month later, William Gadd, a 21-year old working for James Underwood of Hugill, was killed by a fall of earth in Blake Bank cutting, while in the same month a fall of stone in Bowston cutting claimed the life of Joseph Parker.

The potential of the line had already been recognised outside its immediate area. Though all but one of the eleven provisional directors lived in the Kendal and Ambleside districts, the subscribers' list of January 1845 was dominated by outsiders. Some 67 of the 133 subscribers gave addresses in London or the Home Counties, including Thomas Brassey, the contractor. Only 34 were from the K&W's own area. Among these were the directors and Job Bintley, the engineer and surveyor, who had been involved with the Longsleddale proposals and had later worked with Cornelius Nicholson on the construction of the Kentmere reservoirs. Five were from Liverpool, and perhaps their enthusiasm led to the 1844 comment from the *Liverpool Times* that when the L&C and K&W were both complete

Staveley station in the days when it was a manned station, showing the attractive buildings on the up side of the line. In the foreground are the parapet rails of the bridge over the Crook Road. There is a steep climb up to the platform from the road level.
Photo: Harold D Bowtell/CRA Collection

the admirers of this delightful region will be able to reach the banks of Ullswater and Windermere, from Liverpool, in four to five hours. Preparation of what we would now call infrastructure for this expected influx of tourists was already under way. In November 1845 tenders had been invited for excavation, walling, slating and mason's work for an hotel at Birthwaite, by Webster and Thompson, architects. In January 1847 the public notice that the 'Eagle and Child' inn was to be let included the reminder that the K&W railway station in Staveley would be built close by.

By September of 1846 the two companies, L&C and K&W, had completed the line from Lancaster to Oxenholme and thence to Kendal, and this stretch was opened for passenger traffic. Passengers for Carlisle and Scotland continued by road from Kendal, and the service was a great success. *Traffic has exceeded expectations – several of the trains have carried between 60 and 70 passengers,* came the report. The actual opening was made with due ceremony and celebration, as the *Westmorland Gazette* reported:

> *Monday last was a day that will be memorable in the annals of Kendal. Never, perhaps, since the opening of the Kendal Canal, twenty-seven years ago, was the town such a scene of amusement and hilarity.*

> *We were glad to find that Monday last was kept a general holiday, most of the shops being closed in honour of the occasion, for the purpose of giving the assistants, as well as the masters, the opportunity of participating in the festivities of the day. Flags were hoisted on the Town Hall and on the ruined towers of the old Castle, which presents so prominent a landmark to the distant railway traveller, the founders of which little dreamt of the strange and mighty power evoked by science which one day was to sweep round their dismantled place of pride.*

> *It had been arranged that a party of the directors should start from Kendal about eleven o'clock and proceed to Lancaster to join the large train that was expected from that town, but as this arrangement would not allow any of the considerable number of inhabitants of Kendal to share in the trip, it was very properly altered, and a very large number of carriages were brought up from Lancaster. This circumstance delayed the departure of the opening*

train for an hour. In the mean time the temporary station at Longpool became filled with ladies and gentlemen anxious to witness the starting of the first train, a band being stationed on the spot to add to the general hilarity. About half-past twelve eight carriages, gaily decorated with flags, made their appearance, drawn by the new engine, the Dalemain, *and after being duly freighted with ladies and gentlemen passed over the Sedbergh Road and began to ascend the incline, which, at a gradient of one in eighty, unites the Kendal and Windermere branch with the Lancaster and Carlisle at Oxenholme. The distance, which is two miles, was accomplished in about eight minutes. Here there is a very pretty little station, which, like the others on the line, is in the process of completion.*

> *Shortly after leaving Oxenholme an exceedingly pretty view of the town of Kendal and the valley on the west presents itself, which the remarkably clear and brilliant atmosphere of the day displayed to great advantage. The train, after stopping at Sedgwick for a minute or two to pick up several gentlemen, proceeded to the Milnthorpe station, the second on the line, which is a handsome structure about half a mile from the town. The ease and smoothness with which the train proceeded over the new line was the subject of much admiration. The next station is that of Burton and Holme, and passing towards Carnforth station the distant mountain of Ingleborough in Yorkshire, with its broad flat crown, is seen more clearly than we ever beheld it, forming not the least interesting feature of a beautiful ride. Towards Hest Bank, the last station before Lancaster, Morecambe Bay, the dark green waters of which, together with the wooded shores beyond, offered as pretty a picture as could be looked upon. After a few further miles running the train passed over the magnificent bridge across the Lune, which was decorated on each side with streamers, the broad river and the town opposite giving another of the fine effects which the journey offered to the eyes of the traveller. The train, which was driven by G B Worthington, Esq., engineer, arrived at Lancaster fifty-two minutes after leaving the Kendal station at Longpool.*

After waiting about twenty minutes at Lancaster, the train, which was increased to fourteen carriages, proceeded on its return in the view of an immense crowd of spectators, who covered the bridges, the slopes of the neighbouring churchyard and, in fact, every good vantage ground. The return train, a very heavy one, reached Kendal a minute or two over the hour, many of the bridges on the route being covered with spectators. On the arrival of the train at Kendal the sight was really magnificent. The slopes of the Castle hills were black with human figures, and both sides of the line from there to the station were occupied with spectators, including as is quite natural in all matters of sight-seeing, a very large proportion of the fairer portion of creation.

The directors and a number of invited guests then proceeded to the Whitehall in Kendal where at 3pm lunch was served.

About six o'clock the return train started for Lancaster, driven by J C Errington, the engineer of the Lancaster and Carlisle railway, and reached Lancaster in about an hour. About half-past seven the directors of the Lancaster and Carlisle and Kendal and Windermere Companies, with their friends, to the number of about forty, sat down to a superb dinner, given by the directors of the former company at the King's Arms in Lancaster.

The first timetable showed four trains a day in each direction, three of which were 'all stations' to Lancaster. However, the first train of the day, departing Kendal at 3am, was an express carrying only mail and first class passengers and ran non-stop from 'Kendal Junction', as Oxenholme was called then, to Lancaster, taking 58 minutes. Connecting services gave a 1pm arrival in London. A first class ticket from Kendal to Oxenholme cost 6d (2^1/2p), second class 4d (1^1/2p), while the long distance traveller could go to London for 34/3d (£1.71). This is about £68 at present day prices.

Kendal's status as the terminus for the Scotch expresses was short-lived, as the L&C opened fully in December 1846. Meanwhile work on the rest of the K&W continued. In October 1846 the work claimed another life when 'Seedy Jack' Archer was crushed between two laden earth wagons. Later in November a *fine black cat belonging to Mr Parkinson* became the first non-employee of the K&W whose death on the railway was recorded. Out hunting, the speed of the early morning express to Lancaster was too much for it and the unfortunate creature was found *completely cut in two with the mouse firmly fixed between her teeth.*

The company showed some enterprise in attracting passengers. In November 1846 it put on an hourly service between Kendal and Oxenholme on two fair days, no doubt hoping this would persuade country people to sample the delights of rail travel. Goods traffic was also advertised: George Cramley, the Goods Superintendent, published a notice that goods trains left Kendal for the north three days a week, and for the south four days a week. The railway now had the contract for carrying the mail to Oxenholme, and in January 1847 the *Mercury* reported that the railway was having a noticeable effect on Kendal – there were fewer coaches in the town. It also reported an item which gave a hint of problems to come. The winter was cold, and the town ran out of coal, despite the railway facilities. This was serious, especially as one of the benefits of the railway was supposed to be plentiful, cheap coal. There were rumours of *dissension between the Windermere and L&C companies* and the source stated that *a survey of a new line* was in progress. The *Mercury*, however, understood the rumour was *utterly void of foundation* and that *the best understanding subsists between the two companies*: indeed, in February, coaches from Kendal were being attached to L&C trains to *obviate the necessity of passengers and luggage having to change carriages at Oxenholme.* In March 1847 the *Mercury* printed a letter from *Anti-Duplicity* which drew attention to differences between the promises made by Cornelius Nicholson and the reality of the railway. Coal had not come down in price, carriage of goods was not necessarily cheaper (a Highgate trader had paid 10s 10d (54p) for delivery of a box of ribbons by rail, compared to 2s 4d (12p) a year earlier for carriage by canal) and few jobs had been created. However, this seems to have been the voice of a minority.

Finally, on Tuesday 20th April 1847, the great day arrived and the Windermere line was opened in its entirety. Again the *Westmorland Gazette* ran a long report of the proceedings:

Soon after ten o'clock a train of sixteen carriages decorated with flags, accompanied by a band of music, started from the Kendal station with a full freight of holiday makers; and about twelve o'clock another train of eighteen carriages with another band of music followed. These trains were each drawn by three engines, the engines at present in use not being of a very powerful description.

The first point which attracts the attention after leaving the Kendal station, where the line passes through level meadow land, is a large timber viaduct of considerable size, carried for some distance upon massive walls of stonework, placed at intervals, which crosses the River Kent and the race at Dockray Hall or Gandy Mill, as it is popularly called. This viaduct, when viewed from a little distance, presents, with its trellised railings, a very pretty appearance. There are, in fact, two viaducts, one over the stream and one over the race, united by an embankment of earth.

The description continues: *Crossing the road at Aikrigg End over a wooden bridge we have on our right a beautiful view of the valley of the Kent and the little village and chapel of Burneside, with the extensive paper mills.....*

A small station is here in the course of construction, built, like the others, of rough stone of irregular sizes, dark blue in colour, which harmonizes well with the scenery of the district. Here begins a considerable incline of one in eighty. Proceeding in a tolerably direct course towards Staveley, the line traverses a cutting of blue slaty rock of considerable difficulty called the Bowston cutting, and afterwards crosses the turnpike road from Kendal to Ambleside on a level. The thriving village of Staveley presents a very pretty appearance from the railway. The view of Staveley, with its white buildings, is well contrasted with the dark and barren Raven Scar which forms the back ground of the landscape. A short distance further on the little Chapel of Ings is a very pretty object, and on its right, Reston Hall.....

STAVELEY

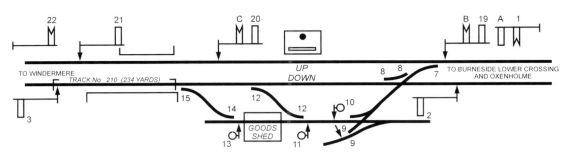

SIGNAL CABIN ~ SIZE 'E' ~ ELEVATION TEN FEET ~ ELEVEN FEET
FROM RAIL ~ SET OF 22 LEVERS ~ SPACES:- 4, 5, 6, 16, 17, 18.

BURNESIDE LOWER CROSSING

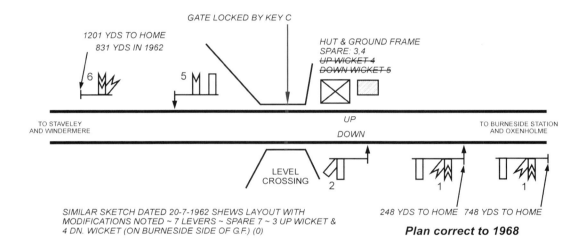

SIMILAR SKETCH DATED 20-7-1962 SHEWS LAYOUT WITH
MODIFICATIONS NOTED ~ 7 LEVERS ~ SPARE 7 ~ 3 UP WICKET &
4 DN. WICKET (ON BURNESIDE SIDE OF G.F.) (0)

Plan correct to 1968

BURNESIDE STATION FRAME

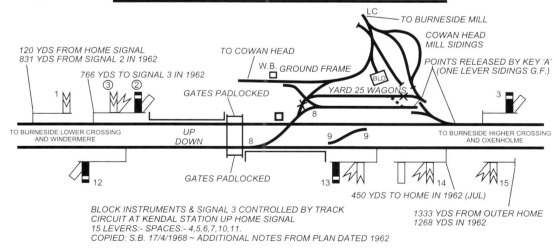

BLOCK INSTRUMENTS & SIGNAL 3 CONTROLLED BY TRACK
CIRCUIT AT KENDAL STATION UP HOME SIGNAL
15 LEVERS:- SPACES:- 4,5,6,7,10,11.
COPIED: S.B. 17/4/1968 ~ ADDITIONAL NOTES FROM PLAN DATED 1962

Plan correct to 1968

LOWER L.C. G.F.	HIGHER L.C. G.F.
219 YDS	430 YDS

BURNESIDE HIGHER CROSSING

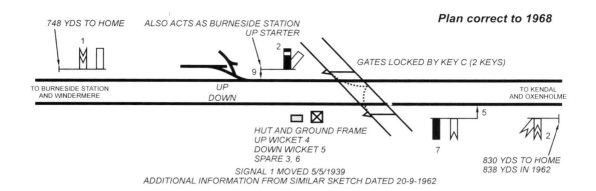

748 YDS TO HOME

ALSO ACTS AS BURNESIDE STATION UP STARTER

Plan correct to 1968

GATES LOCKED BY KEY C (2 KEYS)

TO BURNESIDE STATION AND WINDERMERE

UP
DOWN

TO KENDAL AND OXENHOLME

HUT AND GROUND FRAME
UP WICKET 4
DOWN WICKET 5
SPARE 3, 6
SIGNAL 1 MOVED 5/5/1939
ADDITIONAL INFORMATION FROM SIMILAR SKETCH DATED 20-9-1962

830 YDS TO HOME
838 YDS IN 1962

KENDAL (LNWR)

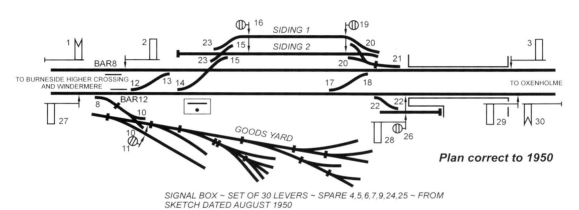

SIDING 1
SIDING 2

TO BURNESIDE HIGHER CROSSING AND WINDERMERE

TO OXENHOLME

GOODS YARD

Plan correct to 1950

SIGNAL BOX ~ SET OF 30 LEVERS ~ SPARE 4,5,6,7,9,24,25 ~ FROM
SKETCH DATED AUGUST 1950

KENDAL (BR)

SPARE:- ③ -18 - 23 ㉕ 30

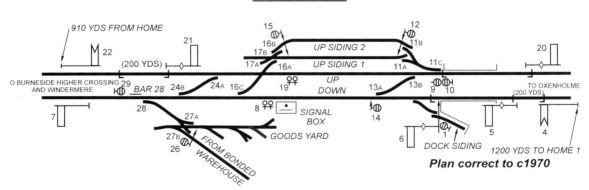

910 YDS FROM HOME

(200 YDS)

UP SIDING 2
UP SIDING 1

O BURNESIDE HIGHER CROSSING AND WINDERMERE

TO OXENHOLME
(200 YDS)

UP
DOWN

SIGNAL BOX

FROM BONDED WAREHOUSE

GOODS YARD

DOCK SIDING

1200 YDS TO HOME 1

Plan correct to c1970

Please Note: To make them more relevant to the text, the diagrams have been arranged in a geographical relationship. They do not use the normal Signal Engineering convention which shows the layout as viewed from the signal box or ground frame.

Signal diagrams redrawn by Alan Johnstone from original information provided by Richard D Foster.

Courtesy Kendal Town Council

Shortly afterwards occurs another cutting of considerable depth and then the line arrives at the summit level, a point from which it descends into the vale of Windermere, and the first view is obtained of the Queen of the Lakes, the effect of this view is heightened by contrast with a bleak moor called Blackmoss, which the railway traverses previously.

On arriving at the terminus the view of the lake gleaming in the sunshine, and then partly hidden behind some wooded promontory, and backed by a fine outline of bolder hills, was magnificent. Although the station is a long way from completion, not being even roofed, an extensive platform has been laid down in front of it, on which the throng of visitors alighted, and thence proceeded on foot or by the numerous vehicles in waiting to the village of Bowness.

Bowness, on Tuesday, was crowded with visitors brought down for the first time by the railway, to the number of not less than six hundred, and great was the run upon the refreshment stores of the inns....

The two steam yachts, the Lady of the Lake *and the* Lord of the Isles, *were put in requisition plying to Ambleside and Newby Bridge with full compliment of visitors.'*

Again the opening was marked by a ceremonial lunch, held in Bowness at the Royal Hotel, at which Cornelius Nicholson explained his hopes for the line:

They proposed to enable the merchant princes of Liverpool, and the cotton-lords of Manchester, to exchange in a few hours the smoke of their factories, and the miasmata of their towns, for the salubrious airs and silver mists that float round the hills they were now among. (Cheers.

The railway will be extended along the shoulders of yonder hill, like a Swiss gallery, carrying it along past the remains of that old king of Cumberland who sleeps on the summit of Dunmail Raise, disturbing his remains, and perhaps scattering his ashes, till we meet other lines which will then give the lake district the full benefits of railway communication (cheers).

Later, at an 'elegant dinner' given at the Crown Hotel in honour of the engineers, Cornelius Nicholson called the line 'the Gem of Railways' and said: *It is a nice railway in an engineering point of view, a cheap railway in an economical point of view, and a beautiful railway in a poetical point of view.*

The Westmorland Gazette concluded its report:

The splendour of the day contributed greatly to the evident enjoyment of all parties and we are glad to add that no accident occurred either by land or lake. Soon after four o'clock the first return train started for Kendal, and at six o'clock a second train departed. Many of the visitors, who had been beguiled no doubt by the charms of the lake, came to the station just in time to see the train disappearing, but fortunately they were ultimately provided for by the special train, which started at nine o'clock..... The trains occupied rather more than half an hour in their return, great caution being very properly exercised.

A railway blessed with such instant popularity, fine views and the prospect of wealthy patrons surely was in for a bright and prosperous future.

3:

A Difficult Independence
The struggle for survival as a small railway company

A busy scene at Windermere in LMS days, a line of empty stock stands in the centre road as a local train is about to leave from platform 2. On the right a 1st class coach stands at platform 1, an addition to the original station.
Photo: Cumbrian Railways Association Collection

EVEN as the crowds were cheering the arrival of the first trains at Birthwaite, there were signs that all was not well. An inquest was held on 20th April into the death of William Constable, railway labourer, who had been run over the previous day by a train at Staveley. Constable had been taken to the house of Richard Beetham for treatment where he had remained lucid long enough to tell Staveley's police officer, William Furness, that it was his own fault. He had been walking along one of the running lines when an engineer's train passed him on the other; knowing the train would return soon, he changed to walking along the other track, but was run over as the train came back on the same line as it had gone up. He died shortly after midnight. Despite Constable taking responsibility the jury noted that the deceased had not been given due notice of the train and that *the arrangements of the company were not such as they ought to be.*

The company's arrangements for attracting passengers seemed in good order, however. People living quite close by took advantage of the opportunity to travel, sometimes showing a lack of knowledge of places not far from their home which we today would think impossible. In May two residents of Troutbeck, anxious to try the railway, took a trip to Kendal. When the time came to return, they got onto another southbound train by mistake and so arrived at Oxenholme *a place they had never seen or heard of before.* They asked the staff the way back to Troutbeck, but a practical joker on the staff gave them directions to Endmoor, and so doubled their journey home.

Local groups were quick to take advantage of the possibilities opened up by the line. Among them were St Thomas' Sunday School, the Temperance Society (who enjoyed a Pic Nic in Mr Curwen's grounds) and the Wesleyan School. The *Mercury* noted approvingly there had been less drunkenness, perhaps due to *the means of rational amusement and recreation which the railway has opened out,* but, on the other hand, the traditional Whit procession in Kendal was abandoned because so many people would be attracted away by the railway. Excursion fares from Lancaster to Windermere cost 8/- (40p) first class, 4/- (20p) second and 3/- (15p) third. Though many visitors came only for the day, others wanted to stay, and on 19th June the *Mercury* reported that there was not enough accommodation in Bowness. The *Mercury* commented *the worst fears of the Laureate are about to be realised, but we confidently anticipate that the result will not be so disastrous as he imagines.* In the week to 12th June a total of 2,625 passengers used the line, including 540 first class, and this figure was to climb through the summer months. In early July Carr's of Carlisle treated 120 of their employees to a trip to Windermere, and a week later an excursion train from Leeds was announced: it would reach Windermere on Saturday and return on Monday. A correspondent, signing himself *Delta,* wrote to the *Mercury* proposing a regatta week on Windermere, with prizes sponsored by the railway companies who could be expected to make a profit by running special trains.

At the first half-yearly meeting of the K&W after the full opening, an operating profit of £727 2s 3d was declared, after allowing for expenses of £2115 1s 10d. This included the sum of £846 5s 6d to the LNWR for the hire of rolling stock, including locomotives. The K&W company had decided not to have its own rolling stock but to hire it from the LNWR, as did the L&C. Cornelius Nicholson praised the K&W as a *cheap line* – it had cost £16,000 per mile to build – and commended the directors on their financial control. When the line opened they had even deducted the cost of their part of the entertainments from their pay. Nicholson concluded by saying that *the best possible understanding subsisted between this company and the L&C.* It was also announced that there were plans to build a church near the Birthwaite terminus which, it was expected, *would attract many gentlemen.*

In some ways the K&W can be seen as a very modern set-up, buying in services rather than being a vertically integrated company which did everything itself. As we have seen, it hired in rolling stock, including engine men and stokers, and it also contracted out maintenance of the track, to Stephenson, Brassey and Co. The K&W supplied guards and breaksmen, and station staff. Whatever the reason, problems soon came to light, particularly in the relationship between the K&W and its 'big brother', the L&C. This is surprising since the two companies shared so much in their beginnings, and Kendal men sat on the board of the L&C. It must have been strange for Mr Wakefield and Mr Cropper (Nicholson's successor at the Burneside paper mill) to receive, in Lancaster, delegations from the K&W including neighbours such as Mr Gandy and Mr Wilson.

As early as 15th October 1847 the chairman of the L&C was to write to the K&W requesting the outstanding balance of the goods traffic account be paid. There were disputes about the rate to be charged for the carriage of coal, and in April 1848 the two companies agreed the L&C would fix the rates, paying the K&W a proportion for its work, counting Oxenholme – Kendal as 4 miles. This seems, on the face of it, generous, especially as the L&C had other grievances, but the goods account was still not settled. The K&W agreed to pay £200 to the L&C to settle the differences between the contract rate and the Clearing House rate up to May 1848. Passenger rates were also fixed at this meeting and were 9d first class from Oxenholme to Kendal, 6d second and 3d third. Then, as now, there were problems with trains making (or missing) connections at Oxenholme. Lateness up to 15 minutes would incur no penalty, unless more than one third were late in a month, when 10/- per train would be payable for any train 10 – 15 minutes late. 15 – 30 minutes late would cost 15/-, rising to 60/- if a train were 45 – 60 minutes late.

In August 1848 another meeting saw the K&W deputation pleading that their line had cost £210,000, but they had only paid £150,000, and thus faced a shortfall of £60,000. They invited the L&C to lease the line for £6,000 p.a., but this was rejected, just as the L&C had said amalgamation was out of the question when approached by the K&W in November 1847. The L&C board wanted to avoid becoming liable for the debts of the K&W, but (perhaps to try to help the K&W out of debt) was willing to consider arrangements of mutual benefit.

Oxenholme was the cause of several problems. Initially the L&C expected the K&W to provide buildings there, but in Juy 1847 it provided a booking office itself; shelter for passengers changing trains was not provided until 1848, and permanent buildings only in 1852. The L&C agreed in July 1849 to pay the K&W £270 p.a. for porters, but only £120 of this would actually be cash, the balance would be in lieu of rent for the K&W booking office at Oxenholme. The Traffic Committee then added a threat, that if the K&W continued to dispute charges for goods, the L&C would set its own rates for goods to Oxenholme, and use its own porters there. They might have done better to take the whole process over, as in August they were requesting the K&W to send as many porters to Oxenholme as it could, and

TIME TABLE.

On and after the 1st of May, 1847.

NOTICE.—The Doors of the Booking Offices will be closed punctually at the Hours fixed for the departure of the Trains after which no person can be admitted. Passengers to ensure being booked, should arrive at the Stations and obtain their Tickets Ten Minutes earlier than the times mentioned in the following Tables :—

UP TRAINS.

Distance from Windermere.	Windermere to Liverpool, Manchester, Birmingham, & London.	1 1st, 2nd, & 3rd Class.	2 1st, 2nd, & 3rd Class.	3 1st, 2nd, & 3rd Class.	4 1st & 2nd Class.	5 1st, 2nd, & 3rd Class.	
	LEAVE	a. m.	a. m.	p. m.	p. m.	p. m.	
Miles.	WINDERMERE	7 0	11 0	12 45	4 50	8 30	
3¾	Staveley	7 10	11 10	12 55	5 0	8 40	
6	Burneside	7 15	11 15	1 5	5 10	8 45	
8¼	Kendal, for North	7 30	11 30	....	5 30	8 55	
10¼	" South	8 10	....	1 25	5 30	....	
	Kendal Junction, for North	7 38	11 44	....	5 37	....	
	" " South	8 20	....	1 39	5 49	....	
	Lancaster	9 30	....	2 50	6 53	....	
	Preston	10 30	....	3 50	7 53	....	
	ARRIVE AT	p. m.					
	Liverpool about	12 20	....	5 45	9 45	....	
	Manchester, Salford Station	12 20	....	5 55	9 45	....	
	" Victoria "	12 10	....	5 35	....	....	
					a. m.		
	Birmingham	3 20	....	7 35	12 36	....	
	London	8 45	....	11 0	5 32	....	
		a. m.	p. m.		p. m.		
	Carlisle	10 4	2 15	....	8 10	....	

* To London and Birmingham First Class only (*Express*).

DOWN TRAINS.

	LEAVE						
Miles.	Carlisle	....	a. m. 6 0	....	a. m. 11 0	p. m. 3 28	....
	London	....	p. m. 8 45	....	....	a. m. 6 15	{ 8 30 { 10 0 }
	Birmingham	....	a. m. 1 25	....	....	11 15	{1 0 {1 45}
				a. m.		p. m.	
	Manchester, Salford Station	....	....	7 15	....	2 0	3 50
	" Victoria "	....	....	7 40	....	1 40	4 0
	Liverpool	....	....	7 30	....	1 30	3 50
	Preston	....	5 50	9 35	....	3 40	5 35
	Lancaster	....	6 39	10 38	....	4 40	6 30
	Kendal Junction	....	7 38	11 45	p. m. 1 39	5 50	7 29
		a. m.					
2	Kendal	5 30	8 30	12 0	1 45	6 0	7 45
4	Burneside	5 35	8 35	12 5	1 50	....	7 50
6	Staveley	5 45	8 45	12 15	2 0	....	7 55
	ARRIVE AT						
10¼	Windermere	6 0	9 0	12 30	2 15	....	8 15

Return Tickets between Kendal and Windermere are granted. Those granted on Saturdays are available to return on the Monday following.

No Trains West of Kendal ON SUNDAYS, at present.

Passengers arriving at Kendal at 7 30 a. m. from Windermere for the *South*, and at 7 45 a. m. from the South *for Windermere*, will have half an hour for refreshment at the Kendal Station.

The Company will not be answerable for any Luggage, unless Booked and Paid for; and for better security, Passengers are recommended to take Carpet Bags and small Packages inside the Carriages, and to have their Address written on all their Luggage in full. Children under 10 years of age, Half Price; Children in arms, unable to walk, pass Free.

The 8 30 A.M. Train from London, and 1 P.M. Train from Birmingham, is a mixed Train, and takes Private Carriages. The 10 A.M. from London and 1 45 P.M. from Birmingham is First Class only.

The first public timetable of the K&W following its opening through to Windermere.

Author's collection

again in September 1850 they were requesting three porters be available for all trains at Oxenholme. In an agreement of August 1852 the two companies shared the cost of the four porters provided for each train; this outbreak of harmony was threatened when, in November, the L&C said it was willing to provide the portering service at half the rate the K&W was charging. This may have been a way of softening the blow of an increase of £50 in the rent, this increase reflecting the L&C's investment of £300 in further public accommodation at the station, which included a refreshment room, let to Mrs. Mason in August 1851 at £10 per annum.

The attitude of the L&C seems to have swung between frustration - in 1850 they had to remind the K&W to return empty wagons promptly, and raised their charges for stock working to Oxenholme in order to be used on the K&W – and a desire to help. They agreed to reckon the line as 12 miles for the purposes of setting excursion fares, and paid an extra 3d for each first or second class passenger booked to or from the K&W other than from the five local stations of Burton, Milnthorpe, Low Gill, Tebay and Grayrigg. Many passenger trains to or from the K&W included through carriages for Liverpool or Manchester which were attached or detached at Oxenholme. The L&C superintendent there could even decide, in the early days, whether or not passengers for London had to change trains, or, if there was not enough room in the London carriages on the L&C train, their K&W coach would be attached to the London train. Any marshalling was to be done by K&W staff under the direction of the L&C superintendent.

It was, however, the way the K&W ran its own trains which really caused problems. In April 1849 the K&W had to be reprimanded for delaying trains as it brought an engine up to Oxenholme for washing out, and in October 1850 the Traffic Committee wrote saying the K&W must *come up to Oxenholme in time to have the luggage carried to the up platform before the arrival of our trains.* Less than a year later, in June 1851, the Traffic Committee was again warning the K&W. L&C trains would depart punctually, without waiting for the K&W, unless their train was actually in the station at the scheduled departure time. Their Oxenholme station master was *specially required to follow out this regulation.*

By November 1853 the L&C board was insisting that K&W trains arrive at Oxenholme 10 minutes before the advertised time of L&C trains, as these were not to wait for the K&W. If K&W trains continued to arrive late the L&C secretary was to investigate arrangements to prevent K&W passengers being left behind.

The Kendal papers too carried news of poor running. In July 1851 it looked as if this would lead to the loss of livestock business. At the half-yearly meeting Mr Foxcroft reported hearing from a butcher in Milnthorpe that, because of delays to trains, he and other butchers were thinking of sending their cattle to Manchester from Milnthorpe, thus bypassing both Kendal market and the K&W. A month later a heavily ironic report in the *Mercury* claimed a train had taken an hour and fifteen minutes for the eight mile trip from Kendal to Birthwaite. On another occasion passengers who were tired of waiting had got out of the train at Burneside and walked to Staveley – and reached there before the train. The L&C's complaints about Oxenholme staff were borne out by a letter from *Go-A-Head*, who contrasted the slick platform work of L&C staff – *Every expedition is used. All the men employed display the utmost activity and the train is off in a few minutes* - with the K&W where *there is not sufficient portering strength.* He blamed the directors of the K&W for being penny-pinching. Perhaps the most spectacular illustration of K&W slowness came in October. A passenger reported that a Kendal trader had met the mail train at Kendal, found and opened his mail, then set off for Ambleside in his gig. He passed the train at Staveley and arrived in Ambleside fully half an hour before the mail. In November 1854 the *Westmorland Gazette* published its own version of the timetable for what had become a *veritable laughing stock*:

On and after Thursday 2nd November, the trains may run as under:

A crowded platform at Kendal station in LNWR days. The co-ordinated way the passengers are arranged looking at the camera suggests this shows a group outing.
Photo: Margaret Duff Collection

The train usually advertised to leave Kendal at noon will, on Thursdays, wait until the Friends' meeting breaks up, in order to accommodate the Friends who live in Birthwaite.

The train advertised to leave Kendal at 3.30 will wait till the goods wagons can be arranged, and may not start until 4 or 4.15.

The train advertised to leave Kendal at 5.15 will, if the rails are slippery, not leave until 6 or 6.15, and in future will stop at Staveley and reach Windermere instead of 5.50, at 6.45. As an additional comfort to the passengers LEAKY LAMPS will for the present be provided in the carriages of this train, and the windows will not be able to be closed, especially as the winter is coming on.

There was some uncertainty about the name of the station where the L&C met the K&W. Timetables published in the Kendal papers showed the K&W running to and from Oxenholme, but the L&C timetable still called this station 'Kendal Junction', as it had been on the first published timetable of May 1847. To be on the safe side a coach proprietor who was running a service to Cockermouth advertised it as departing from *Oxenholme station of the L&C Railway (Kendal Junction)*. At the other end of the line timetables showed 'Windermere' for the station, but even the K&W referred to the area round it as 'Birthwaite'. The *Mercury* referred to 'Birthwaite station' in a report in April 1849 that a post office was to be established there, with station clerk John Garnett as Postmaster.

Throughout the early 1850s the public face of the K&W, seen at the half-yearly meetings, was that all was well, indeed nearly every recording period showed traffic and receipts increasing year by year, but the minutes of the L&C directors show a different story, one of repeated annoyance at the K&W. When in 1853 the K&W informed them it was investigating the possibility of a tramway from Canal Head to the station, the L&C Traffic Committee declined to pay any of the cost, and hoped it would not lead to difficulties between the two railways. The L&C had agreed with the canal company in 1850 that the railway would take the passenger and light goods traffic to Kendal, leaving the coal and heavy goods to the canal. Since the Kendal Gas Company had built its works by the canal, this arrangement kept coal traffic on the canal till the age of road motor transport. The plan for a tramroad was eventually dropped. Later that year the L&C called in the Railway Clearing House to arbitrate over a dispute concerning wagon charges: they claimed £600 from the K&W, but the RCH panel, chaired by Kendal's MP and chairman of the LNWR George Carr Glynn, turned their claim down. However, the K&W directors reported at their next meeting that they had lost out as coal traffic had been reduced because of the dispute. By July matters were so serious that Messrs Whitwell, Wilson and Harrison from the K&W attended a meeting of the Traffic Committee to complain that the L&C had opened a booking office at Oxenholme in competition with the K&W. The two companies' Secretaries and Traffic Managers were instructed to come up with an *amicable arrangement*, treating *the K&W Company as allies of the L&C Company*.

Sadly this was not the end, indeed worse was to come. In order to save costs the K&W gave up its booking office at Oxenholme, and was discovered to be using the L&C's telegraph office instead – at no rent. *They were immediately turned out* noted the Traffic Committee. In August 1854 the L&C gave notice they would terminate the agreement with the K&W over goods traffic to or from Kendal, and distribute it all themselves from Oxenholme. This cost the K&W a lot of money, for even goods marked specifically to be sent to Kendal via the K&W were being off-loaded at Oxenholme. The K&W meeting on 26th January 1856 noted that receipts were down because a *neighbouring company* had changed the system for forwarding goods traffic. This dispute even managed to bring hope of a revival to the canal, for the *Gazette* reported a plan to bring goods from Liverpool to Kendal by water, using ships to Lancaster and thence the canal. The Editor thought the plan should succeed because of the *hostile proceedings* of the L&C.

These repeated arguments so annoyed the tradesmen of Kendal that, in November 1856, a deputation attended the L&C meeting, to report that they had already proposed to the K&W that the two companies amalgamate. The L&C directors replied they were *and ever have been ready to consider any proposition made by the K&W Board*. However, they remained determined to sort things out their way, and later that month the Traffic Committee still went ahead with advertising their own cartage for goods to Kendal.

One of the problems was that the K&W had not, in fact, been as well run as it might. The half-yearly meetings show a constant concern with reducing costs, in particular locomotive power. In January 1850 the directors said they *would not be very sorry to receive such a notice* [from the LNWR, terminating the loco hire agreement] *as they were paying more than they ought*. Later that year they contracted with E B Wilson, the locomotive manufacturers of Leeds for the supply of locomotive power on better terms than those with the LNWR. However, at the February 1852 meeting Mr E Harrison argued that the locomotive department was not providing a proper service: there was *not that regularity which was desirable*. Chairman Mr John Gandy put this down to the change in arrangements, but a year later the directors announced that the contractor would relinquish working the line, and the company would buy Wilson's 0-4-0 tank engines *Langdale* and *Windermere* and some carriages and work the line itself. A third engine, 0-4-2T *Lady of the Lake* was acquired a little later. At this time there was a single road engine shed at Kendal, alongside the present Castle Road, close to the bridge over what was then Peat Lane, now Sedbergh Road, as well as the shed at Windermere. The directors had to spend heavily to put their acquisitions in good condition, but could claim at the July meeting that costs had gone down and punctuality improved since taking over the locomotives. By 1854 they claimed locomotive costs were down to 25% of expenses, a considerable fall from the 61% under the LNWR contract.

Even as they solved one problem, the directors were faced with another. Mr Gandy's confident assertion in 1850 that little money need be put in reserve for track maintenance, because the rails would *last the present generation* without renewal contrasted with the admission just two years later that many sleepers were rotting, and Mr Fell suggested at the half-yearly meeting that not enough had been spent on permanent way maintenance. Action was taken, and a year later Mr Hunt, the inspector, reported that both locomotives and permanent way were in good condition. In 1855, the local Board of Health was concerned about the state of the bridges in Kendal, reporting that trains passing over the Aikrigg End bridge caused a deflection of one foot. Though the company denied this, their Locomotive Superintendent, Luke

Longbottom, admitted that trains did cause deflection of three or four inches on some bridges.

It was fortunate for K&W shareholders that the railway had found a way of cutting locomotive costs, for the mileage was increasing. Northbound and southbound trains were so far from coinciding at Oxenholme that the K&W was running an extra 4,000 miles a year as it sent a separate branch train to meet each main line one. In 1856 it even ordered a new locomotive, a 2-4-0T from Carrett Marshall, *a highly respectable house in Leeds* as Mr Hunt put it, which was named *Grasmere*. By August 1857 the weekday service saw seven trains from Kendal to Oxenholme daily (three of these from Windermere), and nine in the other direction, of which six ran to Windermere.

The railway still encouraged traffic by various means. One was to sell land near the Birthwaite terminus to increase the population, and so passengers, there. In January 1853 the half-yearly meeting heard that part of the Birthwaite estate had been sold to Revd Mr Addison for £3,200 for a 'scholastic establishment'. This estate had cost the company £5,000, but the Chairman pointed out the company still had a good portion of it, worth at least as much, to be sold later if needed. In July 1854, the Company's official report was confident on increasing receipts, thanks to the steady growth in the local population. It noted that *No suspension of new buildings is apparent*, a remark which still rings true today.

Excursion trains brought in lots of visitors in summer. In August 1850, Messrs Gardner & Co. of Preston brought their workmen for a day out, hiring 28 carriages for the trip. Another excursion from Preston ran to 50 carriages, and brought a band along too. Perhaps it was some of these visitors who caused the Bowness people to complain of their rudeness in the *Mercury* a week later. The railway did not forget its local customers: 522 cheap tickets to Windermere were sold in two days to members of Kendal Working Men's Association, and in September 1850 1/- (5p) (third class) or 2/- (10p) (second) bought a return on the 6.30am and 12.15pm trains from Kendal for those wishing to take advantage of the *nutting season*. The K&W co-operated with the L&C to offer excursions to London, giving up to eleven days in town for a fare of £2 5s 0d (£2.25) second class. The advertisements even offered, for a further £2 5s 0d, onward excursions to Paris or Brussels, which must have seemed a miraculous development to people of a small town where, only five years earlier, getting even to Lancaster was a tedious undertaking. In early 1851, a club was formed at the 'Bishop Blaize' inn to organise a visit to the Great Exhibition: the directors of the K&W would put on a special train at a considerable reduction in the fare if they were guaranteed 250 passengers. Those who went to the exhibition were able to see products from Kendal: Messrs J J & W Wilson showed 'railway wrappers', and J Ireland & Co. 'railway travelling and bed rugs'. The spirit of improvement was still strong: in July 1855, 600 schoolchildren were brought to Windermere on an excursion, arranged *to counteract the attraction of Lancaster races*, but alas it rained all day and one assumes the children went home somewhat disconsolate. By 1854 the directors were feeling less charitable about Kendal's inhabitants. Receipts were down, and Mr Kennedy blamed this partly on the cheap fares offered by family season tickets. The Chairman explained *the population of Kendal and its vicinity would not travel by rail to Windermere unless they were taken at a cheap rate*.

Yet despite the bright ideas, and the positive tone of the half yearly reports, all was not well. Publicly this could be seen in the friction with the L&C, and sometimes in accidents due to carelessness. While the company could hardly be blamed for the Birthwaite to Kendal mail train's killing of seven sheep which had strayed onto the line at Dockray Hall Bridge, slack procedures caused a series of potentially very serious accidents at Kendal. A *Mercury* headline on 21st January 1854, 'Runaway train', told how brake failure on a carriage on a down train caused it to run *at a rapid rate through the station* before coming to a halt

An up train from Kendal heads towards Oxenholme alongside Castle Road. The photographer has just passed the site of the K&W engine shed.
Photo: CRA Mayor Collection Ref. MAY 052.

An ex-LNWR **Precursor** *tank brings a train of mixed coaching stock off the K&W line onto the L&C main line at Oxenholme. Photo: H. Gordon Tidey/NRM Collection. Ref. T8345*

on the river bridge: fortunately the line had been clear at the time. The next week the paper reported that the very next day another accident had occurred: another train had run through Kendal station, perhaps slipping on wet rails, and collided with a stray wagon on the main line, causing some injury. The paper commented: *We regret to say that this line is becoming generally notorious for the very inefficient and reckless manner in which it is conducted, and we understand that the company is liable to a heavy fine for running carriages on the line without an engine in front of them.* The Editor also took the opportunity of noting the large number of complaints about *the by no means unfrequent irregularity of their arrival at Oxenholme.* However, the lesson about running without an engine was not learnt. On 13th January 1855 the driver of the last train from Oxenholme was clearly in a hurry to get home. As was apparently still quite common, he arranged for the engine to be detached from the train *not far from the place where the engine shed is situated* about 400 yards on the Oxenholme side of the station. He moved clear of the coaches in order to change lines and back onto the shed, leaving the coaches to coast downhill to the station, in the manner of slip coaches of a later era. This time, however, the engine did not clear the line in time, or the coach brakes were defective and did not slow them down properly, and the three coaches caught the engine up, collided and derailed, crushing the centre coach. All seven passengers were hurt, but none seriously. The crew had leaped to safety just before the crash. After this accident the practice was banned immediately, though the line was later to see other examples of carriages running away on a bank.

Financially, too, there were problems. The K&W £25 shares were often quoted below their face value: in May 1851 they were trading at 9³/₄ - 10 whereas the L&C £50 shares showed a nice premium at 81 – 83. By January 1853 the K&W shares had climbed to 14¹/₂ - 15 but they were to sink lower again as time went on. At the January 1857 meeting Mr John Sharp, a solicitor from Lancaster, claimed to have found irregularities in the accounts. The directors had borrowed £10,000 more than they had had permission for, and the building of the Windermere Hotel by the company was illegal. Replying for the directors, Mr Whitwell defended the extra borrowing by saying it

had reduced interest payments, and the hotel by pointing out it made a profit. Mr Sharp replied that directors' approval did not make the transaction legal. The *Gazette* was perhaps not alone in wondering if Mr Sharp had been sent by the L&C.

If the January meeting had proved difficult thanks to Mr Sharp, the July one was worse. It had to be postponed after a special meeting in June to consider *an arrangement for a lease or amalgamation of the Kendal and Windermere Railway* with the L&C. Mr Rotherham was to arbitrate over the terms of the amalgamation, taking into account the values of each line. In August he proposed that *one thirtieth and thirty-eight decimals* of the net joint income of the Lancaster and Preston, L&C and K&W railways be paid to the K&W shareholders. The K&W directors were acutely aware how their revenue had been hit by the L&C delivering goods in Kendal, and, as they also feared the competition for tourist traffic posed by the about-to-be-opened Ulverston and Lancaster Railway, they were inclined to accept the terms. *Scrutator* wrote to the *Mercury* recommending the terms, explaining the K&W had made no provision for *depreciation or renewal of perishable property* such as wooden bridges, whereas the L&C had done so. Finally, at the delayed half-yearly meeting at the end of August, the K&W directors accepted Mr Rotherham's terms, but only after a long discussion. Thus after just over ten years of independent operation, the K&W did the logical thing and became part of the L&C; however, the turmoil was not yet over, for the L&C itself was to become part of the mighty London and North Western Railway in 1859. The K&W's four engines, *Grasmere*, *Langdale*, *Lady of the Lake* and *Windermere* thus ran for three companies in successive years. Some records show *Grasmere* was renamed *Dwarf* and ran on the LNWR until 1873, others that it was sold to Waring Brothers in 1864. In 1881 it took part in the Stephenson Centenary Celebrations at Newcastle-upon-Tyne, along with other early locomotives including *Invicta*, *Derwent* and *Locomotion*.

Legally the K&W company still existed, and indeed its 4% bonds (renewed at 4¹/₂% in 1855) were renewed in 1860, 1865 and again at 4% by the LNWR in 1870. Both L&C and K&W were wound up by Act of Parliament in 1879 in a tidying up exercise by the LNWR.

4:

The Impact on Windermere

How the railway created a village and gave birth to an industry

Platform 2 of Windermere Station in about 1910. The well-stocked bookstall and the number of staff to be seen confirm its status as a major station. The clock mechanism was housed in the station building and drove the double-faced clock by a shaft.
Photo: Cumbria Libraries/Kendal Local Collection

BEFORE the development of the railway the area which today we know as Windermere village was a hamlet known as Birthwaite. The principal centre of population in the area was the lakeside village of Bowness, which already had some trade as a fashionable spa, having been put on the map by a visit from Queen Adelaide, George IV's widow, in 1840. The development of Windermere village was an accidental consequence of the enforced truncation of the planned line to Low Wood.

The railway company had always intended to attract rich industrialists and their families to live in the area it served, and in this it was successful. To some extent the company encouraged it directly by selling parcels of land for dwelling houses or, in the case of Revd Mr Addison, for St Mary's College. Many of the houses were villas in their own grounds and were built for well-to-do businessmen from the Manchester area, and thus Cornelius Nicholson's prophecies in his 1837 pamphlet were fulfilled. Other, more modest, houses were built with accommodation for summer visitors in mind, and so had attics and cellar kitchens where the locals could live in the summer while accommodating visitors in the main rooms.

The area's attraction was based on the beauty and tranquility of its surroundings, and it attracted mainly visitors who were satisfied with this and did not want the brasher attractions of, say, Blackpool. Nonetheless amenities did develop, most notably the lake steamers. A railway excursion to Birthwaite was frequently followed by a walk down to Bowness and a trip on one of the steamers. The route to the lake was signed by cast iron posts with a gloved hand pointing 'to the lake'. However,

the return route seems to have been more difficult, and New Road was built to give a more direct way to the station – and perhaps cut down the numbers of passengers missing their train home.

Those who preferred to travel further into the Lake District were well catered for by buses and coaches which left from the station itself. The best known of these were Mr Rigg's, who also ran the Windermere Hotel in the early days. His coaches gave visitors the opportunity to visit places which had been praised by Wordsworth and others in their guides to the area, for the great poet himself had been responsible for much of the popularity of his home district. The tolls Mr Rigg and other coach operators paid as they took visitors beyond Windermere to Ambleside were enough to keep the Ambleside Road Turnpike Trust solvent despite the loss of most of its traffic between Kendal and Birthwaite. In due course motor tours were offered, such as those run by Mallinson's Motor Tours from Ellerthwaite Square, who started offering individual tours by car but eventually went into coach tours. This tradition carries on today with firms such as Mountain Goat offering tours to all parts of the Lake District from Windermere.

The permanent residents in the big houses naturally had an immense impact on the service industries in the area. Discerning, or at any rate wealthy, residents or students wanted quality shops to browse in, so these grew up along with business to tempt the servants, for this was the era of domestic staff, both inside and outside. Edward Mallinson, who was Head Gardener for Mr Maxtead at Oaklands, had a staff of forty men working for him. Frank Robinson, better known as 'Franky Fent' of 'Fenty's Album', not only

Local businesses were quick to see the potential of offering rail passengers tours into the central lakes area. An early motor charabanc prepares to leave Windermere station. The driver appears to have less faith in the weather holding than his passengers.
Photo: Margaret Duff Collection

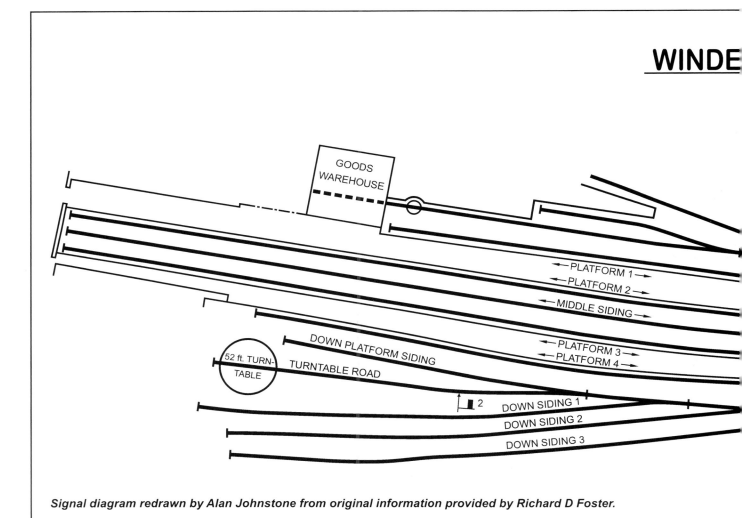

GOODS
WAREHOUSE

←PLATFORM 1→
←PLATFORM 2→

←MIDDLE SIDING→

←PLATFORM 3→
←PLATFORM 4→

52 ft. TURN-TABLE

DOWN PLATFORM SIDING

TURNTABLE ROAD

2

DOWN SIDING 1

DOWN SIDING 2

DOWN SIDING 3

Signal diagram redrawn by Alan Johnstone from original information provided by Richard D Foster.

sold uniforms for servants, but operated an employment bureau through which he came to know who were the lazy servants and the bad employers. One wonders if he was tempted to put the two together sometimes.

Much development in the village was influenced by the Pattinsons, a local family of builders. For the three years from 1845 to 1848, Abraham Pattinson was engaged in work connected with the railway: he built the station itself, the Windermere Hotel across the road, St Mary's Church (built to cater for the growing settlement) and Rectory, as well as the large houses of Craigfoot, for Admiral Sir Thomas Paisley, and Belsfield, for the Baroness de Sternberg. The Birthwaite area was clearly attracting some wealthy inhabitants. In 1846, Pattinson built the two railway bridges near Blackmoss under contract for Brassey and Stephenson. The hotel cost £1,327 7s 6½d, and Abraham Pattinson's account book gives a breakdown of some of the cost:

459 sq. yds. common walling, cellar and
   foundation of principal building   £74 14s 9d
4,149 sq. yds. common wall in principal
   building including offices, walls,
   foundation, chimney and arches   £674 7s 1½d
366 sq. yds. blue flagging   £9 18s 6½d
28 roods of slating   £117 16s 8d

The family firm is still very much part of the Windermere scene, and, in the 1970s, G H Pattinson was the moving spirit behind the establishment of the Windermere Steamboat Museum which keeps alive some boats from the age of elegance on the lake.

As we have already seen, Birthwaite station was used as a post office from 1849, and it was also home to other businesses. An advertisement in the *Mercury* in January 1852 announced that T C Davies of Carlisle had opened a 'Staffordshire Warehouse' at the Windermere Railway Terminus, selling glass and china. Mr W Harrison had his joiner's shop there too, in a section of the building which was not secured at night and served as a meeting place for pipe-smokers after work, and a lodging for tramps. It may have been something left by one of these people which started the fire that broke out at 11am on Sunday 15th May 1853, after the first train had departed.

The joiner's shop and neighbouring blacksmith's shop were destroyed, but Mr Sheldon's horses were saved from their stable, which in fact was little damaged. The station itself was saved by the Kendal fire brigade, brought up by train, and for which one of the railway engines ran a shuttle service to Black Moss to fetch barrels of water. The total loss was reckoned at £1,500, which included £200-worth of furniture belonging to Mr John Gandy, chairman of the K&W, and all Mr Harrison's workers' tools. In a nice display of practical sympathy, the gentlemen taking the train next morning subscribed £50 for Mr Harrison and set up a separate subscription for the tools. A further £10 was collected on the following Sunday when Mr Addison preached two sermons about the fire.

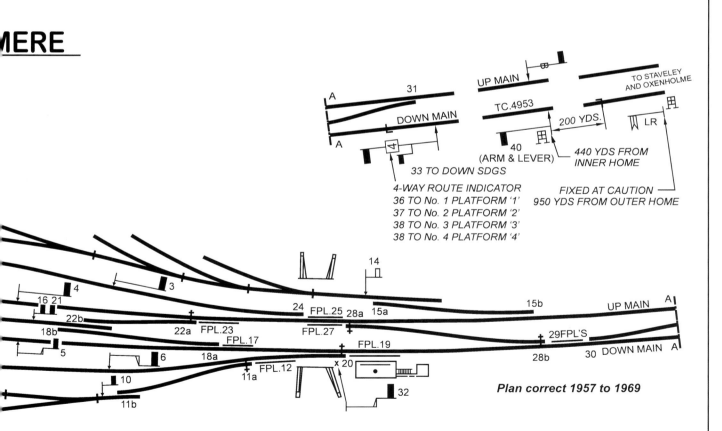

Plan correct 1957 to 1969

GNAL BOX ~ 26'-6" x 12'-0" ~ ELEVATED 10'-0" ~ L.N.W.R. TUMBLER FRAME ~ SET OF 40 LEVERS ~ SPARE:- 1,8,9,13,26,34 & 35 ROM PLANS DATED 2-8-1957 ~ 25-10-1960 ~ 12-10-1967 & 12-3-1969. ~ SIDING CAPACITY - UP SIDE - 69 WAGONS ~ DOWN SDG. TO 3 - 62 WAGONS ~ SPECIAL BELL CODES FOR TRAINS TO FURNESS LINE AND FOR TRAINS TERMINATING AT KENDAL OR OXENHOLME

Census returns for 1841, before the railway was built, show the parishes of Applethwaite and Undermillbeck (which covered the area of present-day Windermere and Bowness) had a combined population of 1,469, which by 1851 grew to 2,085 as the railway began to attract population. Keswick, at the other end of the central lakes' spine, had a population of 2,618 in 1851 (before the building of the Cockermouth, Keswick and Penrith Railway), and this had grown to 4,451 by 1901. In the same half-century Applethwaite and Undermillbeck grew much more quickly, more than doubling in size to 5,061, emphasising the advantage to the area of the K&W line which made it accessible to the well-off for residence and to the less well-off excursionist who wished to enjoy a day in unspoilt nature.

Eventually, the new houses outgrew the confines of Birthwaite, and in 1858 the Post Office decided to name the settlement officially 'Windermere', which would lead in time to the tautologous description 'Lake Windermere'. At the time Leonard Hall was Postmaster, deliveries were made twice a day, though there would only be one on Christmas Day. The railway had the contract for the mails, so it would be collected from the station in the morning for sorting and delivery, and the outgoing mail was taken up to the station in the evening.

Among the wealthy inhabitants of Windermere were Mr Gaddum, a cotton magnate whose house 'Brockhole' is now the National Park Information Centre, and Mr Herbert Coutts of the banking family, whose house 'Hammar Bank' is said to have taken its name from the yellowhammers in the garden. Mr Hedley from a soap-making family owned 'Briery Close', and 'Merewood' was owned by Mr Thwaites from the brewery. Sir William Crossley of the Manchester engineering firm Crossley Brothers lived in the area, as did Sir James Scott, Chairman of the cotton firm John

Above and left - Coach M814, the former Windermere club carriage, photographed at Wolverton in 1957. Though at first glance it looks ordinary enough outside, the interior view shows its unusual saloon design. Photos: Harold D Bowtell/ CRA Collection (both)

A line of elegant yachts on Windermere ready for the start of a regatta in the 1890s. Crews for these boats were often a mixture of professionals (fishermen from Morecambe Bay) and the wealthy amateur owners.

Photo: Cumbria Libraries/Kendal Local Collection

Haslam and Co., and also a director of the Manchester and County Bank. Some of the wealthy came from other centres of industry, including another Crossley family, the carpet makers from Halifax. Sir Mortimer Sladen, whose interest in shipping led him to found the 1st Windermere Sea Scouts, the first Sea Scout troop in the world, was not the only one from this industry: there was also David McIver, MP and a partner in the family shipping firm.

These influential business men naturally used the railway to get to work, and no doubt heard over lunch in Manchester about the success of businessmen from Blackpool in making the commuting more agreeable. They had persuaded the Lancashire and Yorkshire Railway that, in return for them paying a supplement to the first-class fare, the railway would marshal a saloon coach into their regular train, and that entry to this saloon would be restricted to members of the club. The Windermere group set up a similar arrangement and a coach with one small compartment, a large saloon (complete with armchairs, sherry cabinet, a large clock, and a thermometer for checking the temperature) and a cloakroom was put at their disposal. All the travellers who used the club carriage had a first class season ticket, which cost £6 per month, and in addition paid an annual subscription for the privilege of using it. The train left Windermere at around 8.10am - the time varied over the years - and stopped at Kendal before taking the main line south with calls at Lancaster, Preston and Wigan, reaching Manchester Exchange station at 10.30am. The day's work done, the club carriage members would be back at Exchange station for a 5.10pm departure. The return journey was non-stop to Preston, but put in an extra stop on the main line at Carnforth, before calling at Kendal on its way to a 7.20pm arrival in Windermere.

The club carriage users had their own routines and etiquette. At the start of the journey home it was acceptable to talk about business, but at a certain point shop talk was out, and the conversation turned to other subjects, often the prospects for forthcoming regattas, as many of the club members were also keen sailors and prominent members of the Royal Windermere Yacht Club.

This prestigious train with its important passengers, often railway shareholders or directors, received special treatment on the railway. Knowing the club members had their big clock for checking punctuality, and would complain if they were late, every effort would be made by loco crew and signalmen to help it run to time. Comfort was also important: on one cold morning a Windermere porter showed great initiative in avoiding trouble from the club members. On checking the saloon before passengers arrived he noticed the heating had not been connected up as usual. He asked the stationmaster to delay club members on the platform, climbed onto a seat, breathed on the thermometer and so was able to convince his influential passengers that it was not really cold and to give the heat a chance to get through.

The Revd Addison's college did not keep up its early promise and closed quite quickly, but in later years the railway did have a seasonal schools traffic, as students from Charlotte Mason College at Ambleside and St Anne's School used the trains, going to and from home each term, no doubt using all available luggage trolleys on the station to carry their trunks and cases around.

Day visitors were an important part of the traffic and also important for the local economy. Up to 17 excursion trains would arrive on a summer Saturday, with the empty stock being stored as far away as Milnthorpe. The Windermere Institute not only did duty as a dance hall but

Windermere froze sometimes in the 20th century as well as the late 19th; here skaters enjoy the ice in Bowness Bay, probably in the 1920s or 1930s. The tower of St Martin's church is visible on the skyline.

Photo: Cumbria Libraries/Kendal Local Collection

also as a tea room. After spending much of Friday night baking, the women of Windermere would spend Saturday in the Institute supplying home-made teas to visitors.

The steamer service on the lake expanded, and naturally, rowing boats were also available for those who wanted a more active visit. Louis Herbert, of Herbert's Photographic Studio, produced a photograph of the 'Tizzie-Wizzie', a strange creature reputedly to be found on the lake. No doubt many visitors were inspired by the £5 reward offered by the Old England Hotel for the first one captured, dead or alive, to go on a Tizzie-Wizzie hunt. Bowness boatmen reported occasional sightings of Windermere's answer to the Loch Ness monster which encouraged visitors even more.

For much of the time after the K&W reached Windermere in 1847 the town had other railway connections, as the lake steamers brought visitors from the Lakeside terminus of the Furness Railway branch from Ulverston via Haverthwaite. The FR eventually ran its own steamers on the lake, so in LMS days both railways and the connecting boats were part of the same concern, and advertising made much of this. The various reorganisations following nationalisation led in due course to the lake steamers trading under the unlikely title of *Sealink* before they were sold, first to Sea Containers and then to the Bowness Bay Boating Company, bringing them once again into local ownership as part of Windermere Lake Cruises.

Summer no longer sees a succession of excursion trains arriving at Windermere packed with visitors, but instead there are queues of cars and coaches making their way down to Bowness, which is still a very busy place. Wordsworth would probably feel his warnings had been vindicated but it is ironic that nowadays many people look to improvements in the railway to reduce the congestion in Windermere and Bowness while keeping the tourist-based economy buoyant.

5:

The Golden Years

The period under the LNWR and the LMS

A train of 6-wheeled LNWR coaches at the up platform in Burneside. The coaches show many of the different versions produced at Wolverton.　　　　　　　　　　　　　　　　　　　　　*Photo: Margaret Duff Collection*

THE L&C and LNWR had long had close ties, as the L&C had been partly financed by the LNWR, hired its locomotive power from that line, and, unlike the K&W, had not tried to go it alone. Indeed, in 1856, the L&C agreed to buy the locos it was using from the LNWR, which helped the LNWR out at a time of shortage of capital. However, just as the L&C directors had been reluctant to take on the K&W because of the size of the investment they would have to make to bring the railway up to the mark, so the LNWR had the same worries about the L&C. Nonetheless the takeover came and the L&C, now including the K&W, was integrated into the LNWR and given its own local committee.

Though the original Kendal & Windermere shareholders may have had their doubts about the line becoming part of the mighty LNWR, users of the railway soon saw changes for the better. The line immediately gained access to an established company's pool of rolling stock and expertise, which improved the service offered, and also reaped the benefits of being part of an integrated network.

At Windermere, the LNWR acquired a substantial railhead. The station already had a trainshed accommodating two platforms and a centre track, an engine shed, goods warehouse and two plain sidings. In October 1864 the Traffic Committee voted to extend the platforms as traffic had much outgrown the limited extent of the original platforms. Passengers on excursion trains had, on occasions, been alighting in the goods yard and as an interim measure the Committee had, in August, ordered the level of the ballast there to be raised. Eventually two further, shorter platforms were provided using the outer faces of the two original platforms when they were extended beyond the trainshed. The Committee also provided a coal yard adjoining a special siding, turntable, cattle dock and carriage sidings. The passenger station was also improved in 1905 and among the features was a large clock mounted above the main platform, driven by a shaft from the mechanism which was in the station building. Happily this clock is still in the area, having been bought at 'Collectors' Corner' in London by an Elterwater resident. In all, eight sidings were available for stabling carriages, but even so at the peak of the line's popularity for excursions there was not enough room, and carriages would be stored during the day at Staveley or further afield. Strangely, the centre track in the trainshed was never linked to the platform tracks at the inner end, so could not be used as an engine release line. This was one of the reasons for adopting gravity shunting of carriages: the normal practice was for an engine to back its train up the hill where the train brakes were applied, the engine detached and taken to the shed, before the carriages were run down to a platform or siding, controlled by the handbrake. The gradient of 1 in 65 made controlling the speed of a rake of carriages by the handbrake a skilled business, and inevitably things sometimes went wrong. In 1868 a train of eleven coaches, with a brake coach at each end, came in too fast and had a slight collision with the buffer stops. This was not a shunting accident, but a service train which had stopped before reaching the station to detach the engine. There were neither injuries nor damage, indeed Lt. Colonel C S Hutchinson, RE, the Board of Trade's Inspector, reported that the collision had hardly been felt in the rear brake van. He recommended that, for safety, the engine should take its train right into the station. This stopped the risk to passengers, but gravity shunting of empty stock continued and, in the 1920s, a train ran away entering platform 3 and crashed through the buffer stops and station wall, coming to rest in the station yard.

The Branch timetable for May 1875 shows nine weekday trains using the whole line to Windermere. 'All stations' trains to Windermere were allowed 30 minutes for the journey, and 25 or 30 minutes for the return journey. The 12.20pm from Oxenholme had Burneside as a request stop, foreshadowing the arrangement introduced in the May 2000 timetable. The one down 'express' which did not

stop at Burneside or Staveley, also took 30 minutes (4.15pm from Oxenholme, 4.45pm into Windermere) whereas in the reverse direction the 5 pm train fairly flew along, taking 15 minutes to Kendal and another five to Oxenholme. The 8am departure from Windermere offered an 11am arrival at Manchester Victoria, and the 4.25pm return service arrived in Windermere at 8.20pm. The timetable also showed connections or through carriages to London, Birmingham, Liverpool, Edinburgh and Glasgow as well as other destinations. A first class return from Windermere to London cost 74s 8d (£3.78), about £185 at present day prices, to Manchester 25s 6d (£1.27, or £62 today).

On Sundays the line was virtually closed for service trains: there was a train arriving at Windermere at 4.50 am, then a break until the 5.30pm departure for Oxenholme, with a return working arriving at 7.22pm. All-stations trains were allowed 32 minutes from Oxenholme to Windermere, and 30 minutes for the return journey where the gradients helped the train; 'expresses' which did not stop at Burneside or Staveley were allowed 25 minutes down and 21 minutes up. Rigg's coaches connected with seven down trains, sometimes with only 3 minutes' connection time. Mr Rigg must have had great faith in the LNWR punctuality.

The May 1914 timetable shows eleven down trains serving the whole branch, one of which was Saturdays excepted, with three Saturdays only trains, and in high summer 'Saturdays and Mondays only' trains arriving at Windermere at 9.38am and departing 6.55pm. This was a through service to and from London, and there were other London trains which conveyed a through carriage to or from Windermere. The 8.30am (Saturdays excepted) departure from Windermere, which called only at Kendal, and the 7.15 pm return (Saturdays excepted) offered through journeys to Manchester. The return service would call at Oxenholme 'to set down passengers from Preston or beyond' but otherwise only had Kendal as an intermediate stop on the branch. The journey time for these two trains had gradually shortened and eventually they became the 'Club Train' which served the wealthy businessmen living near Windermere, who from 1912 had their exclusive club carriage to ride in as they prepared for or relaxed after the day's business. As early as 1857 the Kendal Chamber of Commerce had asked for the summer timetable 8.45am departure from Oxenholme to become an all-year service

so as to allow persons resident in Kendal to transact business at either of the two towns [Manchester or Liverpool] *and return the same day.*

Windermere also enjoyed the luxury of through services to London. The train which eventually became the 'Lakes Express' in 1927 began as a summer working, but eventually ran at weekends throughout the year. In LMS days it offered a very fast service: leaving London at noon, it arrived at Windermere at 5.25pm, having stopped long enough at Lancaster and Oxenholme for the Barrow and Keswick portions to be detached. In the up direction the train left Windermere at 11.15am, attached the Keswick portion (which had arrived at 11.35am) at Oxenholme, leaving there at 11.53am for a 4.50pm arrival at Euston. The Windermere portion of the train included the restaurant cars.

Excursions remained an important part of the traffic even after the communities of Bowness and Windermere developed. In August 1869 the *Mercury* reported *A great number of excursion trains from various parts of Yorkshire, Lancashire etc. have emptied themselves of large living freight*, the passengers no doubt looking forward to experiencing the beauty of 'the Wordsworth country' as McCorquodale & Co.'s guidebook described the area. On Whit Monday 1883 some 8,000 visitors arrived at Windermere by train. As the process of amalgamation led to the LNWR being dominant in the area, and eventually to the LMS monopoly, the Windermere line was often promoted as one of the gateways to Lakeland. In 1914 cooperation between the LNWR and the Furness Railway (which then owned the lake steamers) led to circular tours being offered. From Lancaster one could travel to Lakeside, then Bowness and return from Windermere, for what seems a very reasonable 3s 6d (17½p). In 1895 a cold snap in January froze the lake, and after the sudden rush of passengers had caused problems – up to 15 people in one compartment - the LNWR profited from this by laying on skaters' specials.

Windermere's engine shed only ever housed one engine. From the 1890s this was a 2-4-2 tank which never went off the branch as it only worked a shuttle service. The shed was closed during the First World War as an economy measure, and for something over a year after this the Windermere engine was replaced by a railmotor shedded at Oxenholme. The railmotor was a small tank engine

In British Railways days, Royal Scot No. 46118 **Royal Welch Fusilier,** *heads an up express passenger train at Kendal.*
Photo: CRA/Mayor Collection. Ref. MAY 047

sandwiched between two third class coaches, which only had slatted wooden seats. The driver had a compartment in the front of each coach, with rodding controls for the brakes and the regulator, and there was a bell system to tell the fireman, who remained on the loco, when to reverse.

After the shed closed, the Windermere turntable remained in use for both regular train and excursion train engines. In order to give the excursion train crews a break, relief crews would come from Oxenholme to shunt the train, turn, oil and water the engines, and have the fire ready for the return trip. With up to 17 extra trains on peak days before 1914, the engine shed would be a busy place. In 1936 the 50 foot turntable was replaced by a 60 foot type which was able to turn the Black 5, Jubilee and Scot classes then in use. The yard staff had been very ingenious in making maximum use of the old turntable; it would take an Experiment class loco with just 1 inch to spare, and

they had turned the longer Claughton class by bolting fishplates on one end of the table so the loco would fit. On the occasions when a larger loco such as a Duchess worked on the Branch, it had to return tender first, and since the Oxenholme turntable was only ever 42 feet long, big locos could not be turned there either.

Traffic increased during the Second World War, as it did everywhere thanks to private travel restrictions. Windermere became the railhead for the Sunderland Flying boat works at White Cross Bay, and also for German prisoners of war en route to Grizedale Hall. Franz von Werra, 'the one that got away', travelled out through Windermere in handcuffs on his way to Canada after his first escape attempt.

Staveley and Burneside, though provided with full passenger facilities such as a booking office and waiting room, were never major sources of passenger traffic.

Oxenholme in LMS days. Note the complicated layout of crossovers, and the line behind the station building giving direct access to the branch.

Photo: CRA/Bowtell Collection

33

On 18th August 1962, Class 5 No. 44709 brings the 1.30pm Crewe - Windermere into Staveley station. All the station buildings in this view have now disappeared.   *Photo: CRA/Bowtell Collection*

Staveley, however, had a special function. Windermere was an open station and incoming trains stopped at Staveley for tickets to be collected. Because of this, the down platform was longer than the up which was used only by local trains. Even so they enjoyed a good service and Staveley village was chosen by some wealthy incomers for their grand residences, though, as Staveley was a long-established village, these new arrivals had less effect than in Windermere.

Kendal was and remains the main centre of population in the line's catchment area and the LNWR tacitly acknowledged this when, soon after leasing the L&C, they rebuilt the station there at a cost of £7,000. However, they underestimated the traffic that would use the station and in 1884 the station was enlarged by the provision of a second platform. Previously trains had often had to wait outside the station until the one platform, for both up and down trains, was free. In its account of Easter holiday traffic in 1882, the *Gazette* also complained that the single booking office window could have been designed to cause a crush, it was so badly situated. After enlargement there were two through platforms, the down one extending onto Longpool Bridge, and a bay platform facing Windermere. This seems a rather curious arrangement, since down trains did regularly terminate at Kendal, whereas few up trains from Windermere did. An underpass under the line provided access to the up platform which also had a stone building, and both platforms had canopies. The three-road carriage shed lay to the north of the up running line (because of subsidence the building was later taken down though the tracks remained), and to the south was an extensive goods yard. Access to this was by a single track which left the running line between the metal footbridge and the viaduct over the Kent. The footbridge still stands, and its length is a testimony to the number of tracks it used to span. Standing on it reveals both the extent of the land the railway used to

occupy, and the significant height difference between the yard and main line. It cannot have been easy hauling a train of wagons out of the yard onto the main line. At its peak the Kendal goods yard had 14 principal roads (as seen starting from the main line):

    two long goods roads used to make up trains;
    two roads leading into the goods shed;
    two short general roads;
    two long roads mainly used for livestock traffic;
    three short roads used by coal merchants;
    two roads into the bonded warehouse which stands
       near the river;
    one road used mainly for oil traffic.

There was also a track which crossed Station Road and led into a wool warehouse, now the Kendal Museum.

Among the trains which terminated at Kendal and did not travel the whole Branch were the Saturdays-only market day trains to and from Lancaster and Ingleton. The Ingleton train had the unusual feature that the loco had to run round its train twice each journey, at Oxenholme and Low Gill, to reverse direction. There was also for many years a regular, direct service to Grange-over-Sands using the Arnside – Hincaster line, with other stops at Heversham and Sandside The 8.55am arrival and 5.50pm departures provided a journey-to-work service for people living in the Grange area and there were trains during the day as well, with an extra return trip on Saturdays for the market. These trains were worked by Furness Railway locomotives and stock in the pre-grouping era.

Kendal's inhabitants used the railway excursions to get away for a day. In August 1868 the *Mercury* reported that the town had been almost deserted on Bank Holiday Monday because of excursions: 384 had gone to Edinburgh, 560 to Leeds and over 500 to Manchester, in addition to those going to Preston, Morecambe or Liverpool. The travellers had a long day of it: *from 5.15am* until *7am the station was thronged with 'trippers'*, but the LNWR made it longer than necessary: *Most of them* [the trains] *returned as they usually do, a few hours after their appointed time.* A fortnight later the LNWR put on special trains, at the very reasonable fare of 2s 3d (11p) return, to Keswick in connection with the Cumberland and Westmorland Show. By comparison with the Bank Holiday trains this was a late start, leaving Kendal at 7.50am.

In addition to the 'Club Train', there was another unofficially named train on the Branch. This was the 'Kendal Whip', the last train of the day to Kendal, which for most of its life left Preston at around 10.30pm, arriving in Kendal after 11 pm. Tradition says it took its name from the need to 'whip in' latecomers to get them home that night. During the Second World War the 'Whip' terminated at Carnforth, but as the engine had to return to Oxenholme shed it is said that servicemen on leave often finished their journey to Kendal in the loco cab. They were only allowed on after the fireman had made up the fire while there was room on the footplate to swing the shovel.

It is difficult now the goods yards are no more to imagine the role the K&W played in freight transport, but each of its four stations was noted for its special goods traffic.

Windermere's exports were particularly varied. Next to the engine shed was the 'gunpowder shed' for the gunpowder mill in Langdale which sent its goods out via the K&W from the early days of the line. Previously it had carted gunpowder to Waterhead to be shipped down the lake to Newby Bridge where further cartage took the gunpowder to the little port of Greenodd for onward transport by sea. Using the K&W offered big savings but even so, the carters could only make one 18-mile return trip daily, taking powder to the railway and bringing back saltpetre. Three or four wagon-loads would be delivered each day, and to minimise the risk of sparks the horses were shod with copper and the wagons had to travel at least 200 yards apart. Windermere's merchandise traffic included fish from the lake, taken to Manchester by passenger train at the rate (in LMS days) of 6s 3d (31p) per cwt. The station also saw traffic in woodworking machine parts from Fells at Troutbeck, Atkinson's Cakes and Biscuits and, from Nicholsons of Bowness, coffins (empty!) for undertakers around the country. Many of these had a long journey, as one of the main customers was Mallets in Truro. Nicholsons also sent out their wood-finishing waxes by train. Coal was of course an important import along with agricultural items such as cattle cake, to feed the stock which would itself leave the district by train later.

Staveley goods yard was smaller than Windermere's, with just three roads, but was also used for coal. It was on the down side of the line and had a small goods shed and cattle dock. The railway allowed Staveley's traditional industry of bobbin making to thrive even when local supplies of timber were used up. In 1873, Fellfoot bobbin mill drew 57% of its raw material from Scandinavian imports and only 3.8% from local supplies. Easy rail access also meant that the finished bobbins could be delivered to the textile mills efficiently. Some of the wealthier incomers imported stone for building their mansions, and, in the other direction, the railway was the export route for slate from the quarries in Kentmere.

Cornelius Nicholson probably took a particularly keen interest in plans for Burneside station, as he owned the paper mill in the village at the time the K&W was planned. He sold out to James Cropper of Liverpool in 1845, and the Cropper family still owns the mill today. Charles James Cropper was a director of the L&C, and as such was one of their delegates in negotiations with the K&W, and joined the LNWR board after its takeover of the L&C. The Cropper family had various privileges on the railway.

The LMS Streamliner Coronation, *at Oxenholme, standing at the K&W platform. The engine has just taken over a train from the Windermere branch. Station Master Raffles stands in attendance*

Photo: CRA/Bowtell Collection

No. 328, Windermere's tank engine stands at Kendal station. This was one of the 4ft 6in. driving wheel 2-4-2 tanks introduced by the LNWR in 1879. Photo: CRA/Bowtell Collection

Burneside station was closed as an economy measure for two years in the 1850s, but as Mr Steele observed at the half-yearly meeting in January 1857, trains stopped there for Mr Cropper's use. He wondered why. *Because he pays us £50 a year* was the chairman's reply. In later years even the club train would stop at Burneside for Mr Cropper's representative, and the station was painted not in LNWR colours, but Cropper's. The LNWR named one of their Claughton class 4-6-0 express locomotives *Charles James Cropper* in 1914, and as a courtesy to the area, used it on the 'Club Train' when new.

Because of the paper mills, Burneside had an extensive goods yard, on the up side of the line on the Kendal side of the level crossing which lay between the staggered platforms. The yard included coal tips, and interchange sidings with Cropper's own tramway system. This system, initially narrow gauge and using horses for traction, consisted of two branches. The shorter branch ran across the village street into the Burneside mill. The longer branch ran alongside the road to the mills at Bowston and at Cowan Head (Cornelius Nicholson was living at Cowan Head at the time he mooted the K&WR). Coal and pulp for papermaking were the main products brought by the K&W and taken on by Cropper's own tramway. In 1924, the tramway was converted to standard gauge, which must have greatly simplified the trans-shipment of wagons, and Cropper's acquired a petrol loco *Rachel* to work it. In 1951, they added a Ruston & Hornsby 0-4-0 diesel loco. Both these veterans went for preservation after the tramway closed, the section to Cowan Head in 1965 and to Burneside in 1972. Some of the tramway rails are still visible near Burneside station, and the Dales Way footpath uses part of the old track bed between Bowston and Cowan Head.

Kendal, like Burneside, had a private tramway at one time, but this one was much shorter. It was in the bobbin mill nearest the running line, and which, in 1891, was auctioned by A Hoggarth and Son on behalf of John Clark. The auctioneer's plan marked an ashpit on the tramway, so presumably it had steam engines. Other buildings in the station yard at the time give an idea of the variety of goods which would pass through. There was a steam saw mill, a marble mason's yard, wool warehouse and brewery.

The steep incline into the goods yard from the running line was turned to good use by the shunters, who would gravity shunt wagons into the different roads. The shunters developed their own system of hand signals to show which siding to use, a system that was handed down from one shunter to another. In summer, gravity shunting could be difficult, as the level of extra traffic through to Windermere meant the shunters could not always back a train up onto the main line for shunting.

The first freight of the day came in from Wigan, usually about 35 wagons in all, and was hauled by an Oxenholme loco. This engine took some of the wagons on to Windermere, and would then shunt Windermere yard, shunting as necessary at Staveley and Burneside on its way back (light engine) to Oxenholme shed. The second freight train of the day brought wagons from Manchester and Liverpool, some of which were for Kendal and again others had to be remarshalled and taken on to Burneside, Staveley and Windermere. Among the Kendal consignment were usually vans which would be sent straight into the warehouse. Kendal's engine shed was closed after the K&W lost its independence, and so at about 9.30am an Oxenholme engine would arrive with traffic from the north and east. This engine would spend the day shunting the yard in Kendal, except for a foray to Burneside at about midday to fetch wagons, and then it would usually bank the Wigan freight from Kendal to Oxenholme, as the 1-in-80 incline was a severe test from a standing start. The shunting engine would then return to Oxenholme shed. Meanwhile the early afternoon goods had gone to Windermere and called at the other yards on its return trip to collect traffic for the north. The usual engines for these freights were latterly Super D class 0-8-0 tender engines. One of these, LMS No. 9151, caused a lot of trouble by derailing regularly on the cattle dock siding. Strangely, no others of the class did this, which was fortunate, since at times there was a lot of livestock traffic. In September there were special sheep sales, and sometimes a train would go from Kendal through to Millom, dropping off sheep at stations on the way, while cattle auctions on Mondays throughout the year kept the cattle dock busy. September was also the time of the Westmorland County Show; before the Second World War most of the stock came by train and was walked up Shap Road to the showground.

LNWR 4-6-0 18 inch goods locomotive No. 8848 on the turntable at Windermere. Notice the gunpowder van in the background - well within spark-carrying distance! Dating this photo presents something of a puzzle. The presence of the gunpowder van suggests a date before 1929, when gunpowder production in Langdale ceased. However, other sources say the loco was only reboilered with a Belpaire firebox (as seen here) in 1933, and withdrawn in 1935.
Photo: Cumbrian Railway Association

Occasionally there were really momentous events in the cattle siding. Two farmers moved their family, livestock and machinery, away by special train, and in September 1904 Buffalo Bill's Wild West Show came to town. Three trains were needed for this: they came to Kendal from Barrow, at a maximum speed of 25 mph, arriving at 3.15, 3.45 and 4.00am. After two performances on the circus field near the old County Showground, the afternoon one watched by 7,000 people, the evening by 8,000, everything was loaded back onto the special trains for departures starting at 1am. The three trains measured 306, 342 and 378 yards in length, and had to be marshalled in precise order, as only designated end vehicles had normal couplings. The yard staff must have had their work cut out managing everything in the time available. Other circuses came by train too, though apparently with less spectacular trains, until 1962.

By today's standards the variety of freight which passed through Kendal's goods yard was amazing. There were not only the independent coal merchants but also the Kendal Equitable Industrial Co-operative Society and later (1930) the Pearson Knowles Coal and Iron Co., Wigan. Cumpsteys tallow chandlers moved to the station yard at the end of the nineteenth century, and imported bones and fat for processing, and, by 1906, were also listed as agents for the Anglo-American Oil Co. Shell, BP and the West Cumberland Farmers also brought in oil products by rail, and there was timber for building work, and sugar beet pulp for use on local farms. Not all trade was inward: Kendal was a busy manufacturing town, and had its staple exports for much of the line's existence. The town had been an important centre for the wool industry, and now exported woollen blankets for the LNWR, Midland and other railway companies, and also shipping lines such as Cunard. Another textile product was carpets, and the railway took out another of Kendal's products, snuff: there were several mills in the town or close by.

The main export, however, was shoes. Thousands of pairs of K shoes were sent off by rail, loaded into the parcels vans which stood in the horse box siding, ready to be drawn out by the station shunter into the carriage siding, from where the engine on the parcels train from Windermere would pick up and attach it to the front of the 6.50pm train to London (initially Euston, later Marylebone). In LNWR days K shoes had arranged a flat rate of 2s (10p) per carton, which covered delivery anywhere in Britain or Europe. A whole section of staff looked after parcels traffic, both inward and outward, and a typical page from the Kendal Carter's Delivery Book of 1875 shows:

> *a bale of bedding from Lancaster for Mr H Wakefield;*
> *a hamper (which weighed almost 1cwt.) from Bristol for Mr Bindloss;*
> *a number of crates and cases of glass from Preston for C Shufflebottom;*
> *a case of food from Maryport for Dodd;*
> *a parcel from Skipton for Barrington;*
> *two bags of food from Huddersfield for J. Pennington;*
> *a package from Windermere for Hudson.*

For the delivery of parcels there were horse-drawn carts based at the station which, like Windermere, had its own stables. In the 1930s, motor vans were used for parcels distribution outside the town, leaving the shorter distances to the horses until 1950, when motor vans took over even this traffic.

Oxenholme occupied a special position in the life of the K&W as it was there that the branch met the main line; some of the problems of this interface in early days have been described. Staff there probably soon benefited from the takeover of the K&W by the L&C as this put an end to the rivalry between the operators of the branch and of the main line. For most of the history of the branch there was much shunting at Oxenholme of through carriages, entailing the splitting and joining of trains en route. The track layout at Oxenholme accommodated this operation, with two sets of points giving access to the branch, one at each end of the station. Trains could run straight onto the branch by leaving the main line south of the station and either running into platform 3 or taking the through line that ran behind the station wall. (The branch platform, number 3, was, and is, often referred to as the 'bay platform', though it is in fact a through line.) Alternatively a train could draw up in platform 2 and then move onto the branch; this would be the case for trains such as the 'Lakes Express' which split at Oxenholme. One consequence was that long northbound trains would have to draw up twice at Oxenholme, the platform not being long enough to take the whole train. Trains leaving the branch could take either the main line, using the intricate crossovers at the north end of the station,

Oxenholme engine shed in LMS days. A Fowler tank stands in the foreground, with two ex-LNWR Bowen-Cooke tanks beyond. Oxenholme supplied bankers for the main line as well as engines to work the branch.

Photo: CRA/Bowtell Collection

or platform 3, or the through line outside the trainshed. Oxenholme had, and still has, elegant stone-built buildings on the up side of the line, and all three platforms had canopies. Platform 3, for the branch, also enjoyed protection from the prevailing wind and frequent rain which was afforded by the high wall and overall roof at the west side of the station. These buildings date mainly from the 1881 rebuilding, which also diverted the Kendal – Kirkby Lonsdale road from its level crossing at the south end of the platforms to an overbridge a few hundred yards further south. The subway connecting the platforms was built on the site of the former level crossing. The new arrangements certainly improved safety for passengers. In December 1862, a Mr Shaw had fallen into an ashpit while crossing the line at Oxenholme, and the company had to pay compensation. The branch never had a direct connection to the northern section of the main line, so the market day trains for Ingleton had to run into platform 2 so that the engine could run round its train for the journey to Low Gill.

There were goods facilities at Oxenholme, including a cattle dock and warehouse, but Oxenholme was never a major source of goods traffic to the railway. It was, however, important as the place where freight and parcels traffic from the branch would be attached to long distance trains for onward transit.

Oxenholme was probably most noted for its engine shed, because right up to the end of steam many trains needed banking assistance up the hills towards Grayrigg and Shap. The shed itself was rebuilt and enlarged in 1880, when it had four roads, a coal stage and turntable. As the turntable was only 42 feet long, it was fine for turning the 0-6-0 tender engines of early days or the 2-6-4 tanks which were the main bankers in later years. Oxenholme provided the daily shunting engine for Kendal, and locos for the local trains on the branch, and Oxenholme crews would often take 'foreign' engines over for the trip down the branch. The junction layout of some complexity needed, at first, three signal boxes. This was reduced to two in 1943: No. 1 box by the Burton Road bridge; and a new No. 2 box, at the south end of platform 1, replacing the previous No. 2 and No. 3.

Thus, for almost a century from the absorption by the LNWR through to the grouping and LMS days in the 1930s, the Kendal and Windermere Railway played a leading role in the life of the area it served, transporting residents and their goods, and bringing visitors who made an increasing contribution to the area's economy.

6:

An Environmental Interlude

Changes in attitudes to the railway during its lifetime

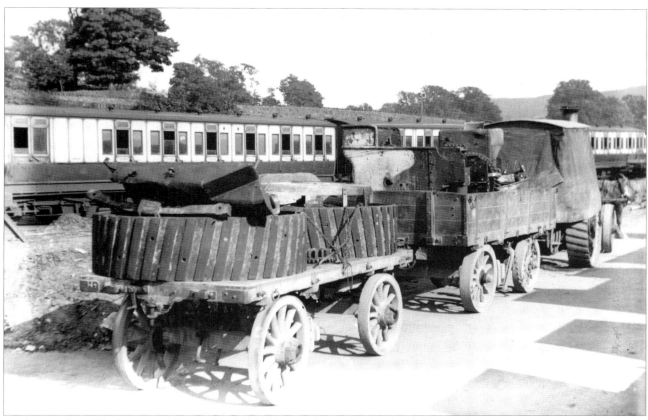

A scene from Windermere station yard in 1894. The traction engine has hauled parts of a contractor's engine, salvaged after it fell into Thirlmere during the construction of the Manchester Corporation reservoir there.

Photo: Abbot Hall Art Gallery. Ref. 239

GIVEN the success of the Windermere Railway, at least once it enjoyed the competent management of the LNWR, it is not surprising that schemes to extend it appeared. Even in the 1840s there had been plans to link the Windermere end of the line to other railways, though these plans had not progressed beyond the early publicity stage. However, the completion of the Cockermouth, Keswick and Penrith Railway in 1865 made the idea of a Windermere – Keswick link particularly attractive.

When the first of these projects was mooted in 1875 there was widespread opposition which showed how much public opinion had changed since Wordsworth's day. While in the 1840s his had been almost a lone voice in favour of protecting the peace of the district, now there were many influential figures advancing arguments rather similar to Wordsworth's of thirty years earlier.

Most prominent among these was John Ruskin, the noted art critic, painter and supporter of the dignity of the artisan craftsman, who lived at Brantwood, overlooking Coniston Water. Encouraged by Robert Somervell of Hazelthwaite, Windermere, Ruskin contributed an article to Somervell's protest pamphlet, which also included a petition form for sympathisers to fill in. Somervell feared the Ambleside Railway would *turn the country of*

Wordsworth into a Black Country, and echoing the great poet wanted to keep away those who did not appreciate the Lake District's beauty: *the majority of the persons composing them* [the crowds] *are bored by our fine scenery.* His pamphlet had wide circulation and, on 22nd January 1876, the *Saturday Review* quoted from it: *If the ascent of Helvellyn or Fairfield had to be begun amidst the smoke of chimneys, the roar of furnaces and the shrieks of railway engines, the special charm of the Lake Scenery would be gone.* Ruskin himself was as rude about the crowds of tourists as Wordsworth had been:

> *The stupid herds of modern tourists let themselves be emptied, like coals from a sack, at Windermere and Keswick. Having got there, what the new railway has to do is to shovel those who have come to Keswick, to Windermere - and to shovel those who have come to Windermere, to Keswick. And what then? All that your railroad company can do for* [the tourists] *is only to open taverns and skittle grounds around Grasmere, which will soon, then, be nothing but a pool of drainage, with a beach of broken gingerbeer bottles; and their minds will be no more improved by contemplating the scenery of such a lake than Blackpool.*

LMS standard Fowler 2-6-4 tank engine, No. 42313, leaves Oxenholme for Windermere with a train of carriages in early British Railways crimson and cream livery.

Photo: CRA/Mayor Collection. Ref. MAY153

The scheme foundered on costs and discouraging traffic projections rather than the conservationists' protests, but their action in advancing conservation issues against commerce and enterprise was an important milestone in the development of what today we would call the environmental lobby. Equally, however, we could view it as an early example of 'nimbyism'. In his biography of Robert Somervell, his son David wrote: *In the early fifties the making of the Windermere branch enabled my grandfather [R M Somervell, the founder of K Shoes] to move out in the country, nine miles away, and yet remain within half an hour's journey of his place of business.* The family had clearly been willing to use the railway to their advantage, but twenty years later spearheaded the opposition to an extension which would have passed close to their home of Hazelthwaite, on the Ambleside Road.

When another proposal for a railway through Ambleside was put forward in 1886 the Lake District Defence Society - formed partly as a result of the 1875 plans - with its Secretary, Canon Rawnsley, was quick to organise protests against this planned intrusion into the *splendid natural scenery*. Among the arguments considered by the House of Commons committee were some emphasising how the line would open up more of the District; the railway would put Rydal and Grasmere within the reach of those wanting to spend a day in the hills and then return home. This was an echo of arguments for the recreational benefits of the

Lake District put forward by Nicholson and his supporters three decades before. On a more mundane economic note, Mr Perks, of the Elterwater Gunpowder Works. explained he would save 50% of his cartage costs as each cart would be able to make two daily return trips to a station at Ambleside, as against one to Windermere. In the end, however, the scheme was shown to be impracticable when the LNWR declined to operate the line.

Eventually the LDDS under Canon Rawnsley was one of the main spurs to the formation of the National Trust, which today is a major landowner in the Lake District, and so the railway to Windermere and the unsuccessful attempt to extend it can be said to have been a major influence in the conservationist movement in Britain.

There were later proposals for extensions, for the Ambleside Light Railway in 1896, for a 3ft. 6in. gauge electric tramway from Bowness to Ambleside in 1899, and, in the twentieth century, for an Ambleside – Keswick line with petrol-electric traction. In 1994 there was a further proposal, for a single track line from Windermere to Keswick and on to Cockermouth and Maryport. It is a sign of the change in public attitudes that, whereas the earlier schemes were turned down because of the impact of a railway on the scenery, the 1994 one was proposed as an improvement to the environment since, it was claimed, it would reduce car traffic, which has become one of the most difficult problems in the Lake District. However, despite this claim to environmental benefits, the scheme did not go ahead.

7:

A Slow Decline

The first quarter century of Nationalisation

The main entrance to Kendal station in early British Railways days. The Scamell* Mechanical Horse *parcel van parked at the top of the yard is a reminder of the railway's important role in parcels distribution in those days.

Photo: National Railway Museum/L&GRP 27161

NATIONALISATION following the Transport Act of 1947 had little immediate impact on the branch. It was well within LMS territory and the local organisation remained much as it had been. The service pattern was recognisably similar to pre-war days, though average speeds were often lower and some of the finer trimmings had disappeared. The club carriage, for example, had been taken out of service during the war, probably at the time the LMS withdrew most of its restaurant car services, and never reappeared on the train. The club members were, however, spared complete austerity, as the LMS provided an open first coach with 36 seats arranged in fours and twos at tables for the train. In the 1950s a slightly larger ex-LMS open first was provided, marshalled second from the engine on leaving Windermere, and a group of regular travellers maintained something of the club tradition in this coach. The train staff helped by guiding other first class passengers to a compartment in the 1st/3rd composite coach further down the train. This shadow of the former 'Club Train' ceased to run in 1966, and by 1969 there were no through trains to Manchester; instead travellers had to change at Preston.

The 'Lakes Express', the other well known long distance train on the branch, fared better than the 'Club Train'. It continued to run as a prestige, named train from Euston with portions for Windermere (which included the restaurant and buffet cars) and Workington via Penrith and Keswick. Through the summer timetable this ran

each weekday, (Saturdays excepted), and in winter timetables there were through carriages to London (leaving Windermere at 9.25am in 1962-3) and Crewe (11am from Windermere)

The direct service to Grange had stopped during the war and was not reinstated. As well as a significant loss for Kendal, since it meant travelling to Carnforth or Lancaster to change to a Barrow line train, the loss of this service must have contributed to the eventual decision to close the Arnside – Hincaster link on economic grounds. Bus services were not an attractive substitute until the introduction of a subsidised express link between Kendal and Barrow via Grange in the late 1990s.

As the post-nationalisation standardisation and 1955 modernisation plans got under way there were changes to the stock which worked on the branch. The 'Club Train', however, still usually had an ex-LMS loco, 'Scot', 'Baby Scot' or 'Jubilee' classes predominating. It was a Jubilee which was credited with a post-war record slow time of 1 hour 20 minutes for the $6^{1}/_{4}$ miles from Burneside to Windermere with the return 'Club Train', having a lot of difficulty with leaves on the line, and thus showing that this now-notorious cause of delay is not a 1990s phenomenon. The morning 'Club Train' was usually pulled by the loco which had worked the morning mail to Windermere, so if this incoming train was late a humble Oxenholme tank engine would take the train, probably as far as Preston, the nearest depot with spare express passenger engines.

Excursion traffic continued into the diesel era. Jubilee No. 45699 Galatea, stands in platform 3, Class 4 2-6-4 tank No. 42571 waits at platform 2 with a local train, and an English Electric Type 4 1-Co-Co-1 is at platform 1. Photo: CRA/Bowtell Collection

There are records of Pacifics working the branch: for example 'Clan' No. 72006 took the 'Club Train' at least once, and 'Britannias' and 'Duchesses' were recorded occasionally on various trains. The 'Lakes Express' would also bring larger than usual engines onto the branch: Class 40 diesels appeared on this train and the winter through London service. Eventually, Class 50 diesels also visited Windermere, often with excursion trains.

Through the 1950s and 1960s there was a gradual decline in traffic, though the branch still carried large amounts of certain goods and parcels traffic. John Cottam, station foreman at Kendal from 1965–71, remembers the hard work it was to load the parcels in time for the scheduled 6.35pm departure. The parcel vans were loaded on the up platform, and so, whenever an up service was due, the vans had to be shunted out of the way, then brought back. He recalls delivery vans from K shoes and the GPO queuing in the forecourt while the station staff checked off the parcels. Livestock traffic dwindled and eventually disappeared, but coal remained a significant import, with coal dumps at all four branch stations.

Oxenholme shed closed in 1962. Banking engines were sent down from Tebay until that shed closed, and then from Carnforth, one of the last steam depots in operation on British Rail. The need for banking engines in any case diminished with the coming of the diesels. The Windermere branch was one of the last to see steam in service: Stanier 5MT No. 44984 was photographed shunting at Windermere on 1st August 1968, a matter of hours before the official end of steam on BR.

Later, diesel multiple units were used on the branch for local passenger services, a change which avoided the need to shunt the train at Windermere. This must have been quite a relief as, on a fine day in August 1962, yet another runaway accident occurred. The carriages from the summer-only Blackpool – Windermere train had, as usual, been propelled out of the station up the hill towards Black Moss, the engine being detached to run down to the turntable for attention. The carriages were then gravity-shunted into platform 3, the one opposite the booking office in the trainshed. Despite the efforts of the shunters in the two end coaches, the handbrakes were unable to stop the coaches in time; the two men leapt to safety before the train crashed through the buffers and made a hole in the wall behind. Fortunately nobody was hurt, though it could have been so different – the area where the coach crashed was often used in bad weather by passengers waiting for buses.

On the freight side the fall-off in traffic meant that in the early 60s there were just two daily goods trains which ran through to Windermere, and no Kendal-only goods trains. Eventually this was reduced to one daily freight service, which carried mainly coal. Burneside closed to general goods in 1964 and Cropper's tramway to Cowan Head closed the next year. Coal deliveries for Cropper's continued until 1972 and the coal was ferried across to the mill by the short private line.

Windermere station in the days of the first-generation diesel multiple units. The photograph, taken on 10th June 1972, shows clearly the extensive ironwork of the overall roof covering platforms 2 and 3.
Photo: Peter W Robinson

The spectacular results of the August 1962 crash, when a rake of coaches ran away down the bank into Windermere station. Despite the extensive damage, nobody was hurt. Photo: Ron Rimmer

Windermere station during its decline. Platform 2 is still in use, and passengers can still shelter under its roof. On platform 3 the lamp standards have been taken down ready for clearance. Photo: Harold D Bowtell/ CRA Collection

Demolition of Kendal station under way in February 1974, in the first winter after the line was downgraded to a 'long siding'. The current platform shelter stands where the big girders lie. Photo: Geoffrey Allonby

A Birmingham RC&W 'Calder Valley' unit on an excursion, at Oxenholme. The destination board suggests it is on the return journey.
Photo: CRA/Bowtell Collection

Staveley also closed to goods traffic in 1964, Windermere following in 1969, leaving such goods traffic as remained to be dealt with at Kendal. There was understandable annoyance at Windermere, especially among the coal merchants who were forced to collect coal from Kendal, particularly as the sidings in Windermere goods yard remained in situ till 1972. Within a year the coal merchants faced an even longer journey, as Kendal goods yard was closed in 1970.

Alongside the cutbacks in service were measures to save money. The track layout at Windermere was simplified in 1971 so that four tracks remained usable, with consequent simplification in the signal box. Burneside and Staveley signal boxes had for some time been closed in winter, as the reduced traffic could be dealt with adequately with the line divided into just two section, one controlled by Windermere, the other by Kendal. In the early 1960s

summer traffic still needed the Burneside and Staveley boxes in use in order to permit more trains on the line. However, Staveley signal box closed for good on 30th May 1964. In 1967 the level crossing at Staveley, the busiest on the line as it was then on the main road from Kendal to the Lake District, was converted to automatic half barrier operation. Burneside Higher crossing remains a manually operated gated crossing, and now is the only signalling point on the branch, having signals to protect the crossing. For this reason the crossing-keeper has been upgraded to signalman status.

The branch was, of course, by no means alone in its decline, and in fact was faring better than others in the area. The Lakeside branch closed to passenger traffic in 1965, thus ending the inclusive rail and boat circular tours which had been a feature of railway companies' summer traffic for many years. When the Penrith – Keswick line closed

Even after the goods yard tracks were removed Windermere still saw some impressive trains. An English Electric Class 50 waits at platform 1.
Photo: CRA/ Mayor Collection Ref. 065

in March 1972 the Windermere branch became the last line running into the Lake District, but its own future looked anything but secure. With all freight traffic gone, much of the goods yard land was sold for building: at Windermere the up side yard area was bought by Lakeland Plastics, now Lakeland Limited, in Kendal the Beezon Road industrial estate grew up on the former goods yard, while trade units were also set up at Burneside. Miller-Turner Printers named their design arm 'Blackline' in recognition of the situation of their works, built on former coal sidings at Kendal. In 1971, Kendal joined Burneside and Staveley as an unstaffed station. Through running between Windermere and London ceased in 1970, and the service from Oxenholme was now but a shadow of the great days. As electrification of the West Coast main line north of Crewe went ahead there were calls for the branch to be included, but what in fact happened was severe downgrading. The branch was reduced to single track from May 1973 and Windermere, Kendal, Burneside and both Oxenholme signal boxes closed. The branch was now in effect now a long siding worked on the principle of one train only at a time.

The signal which protects the branch is controlled from Carlisle, as are all the signals at Oxenholme. The big crossover at Oxenholme which enabled trains to run directly onto the branch from the main line had been taken out in 1968, leaving the track through platform 3 as the only access after the track which ran behind the station wall was taken up. There was a bonus for the mainline trains in the new arrangement, as platform 2 was extended further north and trains no longer need to draw up twice. During the singling BR took the opportunity of easing some of the curves, using the down platform at Kendal and the up platform at the other three stations. The remaining track within a now sad looking Windermere station was shortened, so the first sign to greet passengers was: 'Please join the train 100 yards down the platform'. It was, of course, now impossible to run excursion trains on the branch as the service train occupied it, but as there had been only 14 excursions in the whole of 1972 – in the great days as many came in a single day – this did not seem a problem at the time. At Burneside and Staveley the unused platform was allowed to decay, while at Kendal the up platform and its buildings were demolished, as were the station house and offices at Staveley. Kendal station buildings were boarded up and soon started to look seedy, and might well have been demolished had the planning authority not redrawn the Kendal Conservation Area boundary to include it. The line was truly a shadow of its former self and it seemed to many observers that it faced an uncertain and probably short future.

Cropper's Burneside Tramway

Top
The Ruston & Hornsby diesel loco, bought by Cropper's in 1951 for use on their tramroad, stands in the Burneside Mill sidings, its driver Bruce Ireland in the cab.

Photo: Alan Sykes

Below
Cropper's first standard gauge loco Rachel, a 90hp petrol engined product of the Motor, Rail and Tramcar Co., pauses on its journey along the tramroad to Cowan Head.

Photo: Cumbrian Railways Association Collection

The rails of Cropper's tramroad to Cowan Head at the point where the track left Burneside station yard.
Photo: Peter W Robinson

8:

Revival and Partnership

Sectorisation, Privatisation and Community Involvement

Windermere station in its present form. Booths supermarket occupies the site of the former station building, and on the foreshortened former platform 2 stands the new booking office and waiting room.

Photo: Harold D Bowtell/ CRA Collection

BY THE early 1980s, the Windermere branch was the lone survivor of the many minor railways which had existed in Cumbria thirty years earlier. It survived thanks to the cumulative effect of several reasons. It had a fair-sized population in its own area, so saw local and outward travel as well as tourists, unlike, say, the Lakeside branch which served a thinly populated area. It had the advantage of the direct main line connection at Oxenholme and the relatively short journey from there to Windermere. The Keswick line had enjoyed similar benefits, but the Windermere line had one cost advantage. As Cornelius Nicholson had observed in 1847, it was a *cheap railway* with relatively little expensive civil engineering to maintain.

If one event can be said to have sparked off a revival, it was the 1980 announcement that what remained of Windermere station would be sold to a supermarket chain, while the remaining, shorter platform would have a small prefabricated booking office on it, with minimum facilities. Local residents and councils had protested at each stage of the earlier cutbacks to no avail, but this time it was different. A group of people came together in early 1984 and formed the Lakes Line Action Group. Their first campaign was to press for a larger station building at Windermere, to a design in keeping with its status as railhead for and in the Lake District National Park. Eventually a partnership between the Action Group and local councils and businesses raised £15,000 as a contribution to a new building, and this persuaded British Rail to opt for the present building with its ticket office, waiting room and sheltered waiting area.

The new station was opened on 17th April 1986, and since then has regularly won awards in 'Windermere in Bloom' – the Action Group supplies bulb tubs and hanging baskets each year - and it was even featured in 'Jane's World Transport Systems'. In 1991 and 1992 Windermere station won the regional 'Best Kept Station' award. The original station was bought by Booths, a regional supermarket chain, and converted into a new store with its car park on what had been the engine shed and turntable area on the down side of the line. The silhouette of the supermarket is similar to the old station's, and the colonnaded porte cochère, mentioned in most descriptions of the station, is still there, now in use as the fruit and vegetables department goods entrance. The station forecourt has a taxi rank and bus stop area, so making interchange between rail and bus easier; the passenger information screen lists both bus and rail departures. In recent years a cycle hire business has been set up at the station, offering discounts to hirers who arrive by train, and even through 'train + bike' tickets.

The Action Group's next targeted station was Kendal, which was scheduled to have just a bus-shelter type of platform building. Here BR's architects decided to build a stone shelter with pitched roof, again with a financial contribution from the Action Group, and this was opened in 1991. In the meantime, plans for the station building's conversion into offices were going ahead, and eventually most of the building became Station House Surgery. Patients sitting in the waiting area can both feel and hear the train rumbling by, and as a link with the past the London

The delayed 09.53 to Manchester at Kendal on 7th February 1996. Heavy snowfall on 5th and 6th caused serious disruption to services, but by 7th the rail service was almost back to normal despite the low temperatures and lying snow.

Photo: Author

Midland Region maroon station nameboard is permanently displayed in the surgery foyer. The surgery car park is reached by the subway under the track and occupies the area of the former up platform, while passenger access to the station is by the ramp which led to the bay platform.

Staveley and Burneside station both have a small shelter for passengers and a phone by which passengers can obtain information about train running. In 1988 the long-awaited Staveley bypass was built, to give relief to the villagers. Thanks to the prompting of the Action Group, whose chairman, Colin Reynolds, was at the time a District Councillor, the bypass bridge over the railway took account of possible future growth: it was made wide enough to accommodate double track and high enough to allow for overhead electrification. In November 1999, the track under the bypass was the first part of the branch to be relaid with continuous welded rail.

At Oxenholme station the wall which held up the western end of the canopy over platforms 2 and 3, and protected against the south-west wind, began to show signs of old age, and in 2000 Railtrack began a comprehensive refurbishment programme. This involved a new stone clad reinforced concrete wall being built, new glazing fitted to the platform canopies, and the ironwork painted. An earlier, less extensive refurbishment of the buildings on platform 1 in 1991 created a tasteful booking office and pleasantly airy waiting room, winning a commendation in the 1992 Ian Allan Heritage Awards and later the 'Best dressed station' award in 1999 from the Business Manager North.

The service on the branch has improved and indeed has now reached virtual saturation point for the layout bequeathed by the costcutters. The service is now roughly one train each way per hour from 06.30, with some longer gaps in the evenings. For many years the last train on Friday and Saturday has gone from Windermere to Lancaster, then to Morecambe and finally to Barrow, using the Bare Lane – Hest Bank chord, the only regular use of

this short stretch of track and, from a photographer's point of view, sadly always in the dark. Encouraged by the Action Group, Regional Railways introduced more suitable rolling stock which catered for the large number of visitors with luggage, and, as Oxenholme was now enjoying a good service to London, the branch came into its own as a feeder route. Electrification brought not only faster but more regular West Coast and Cross Country services, nearly all of which stopped at Oxenholme. In the later 1990s even the northbound Royal Scot did so, which meant London to Windermere could take a little over 3$^{1}/_{2}$ hours.

There were occasional reports that the branch would be electrified; in October 1984 this was expected within 18 months, but it was not to be, even though the cost was to be kept down by re-using equipment salvaged from Carlisle's Kingmoor yard. In 1988 modernisation at Oxenholme included passenger information screens and a long-line public address system at Kendal so that Oxenholme staff could inform passengers at Kendal of changes to train running. The Windermere branch itself was now being marketed as the Lakes Line, taking the name from the Action Group. The Group, finding the 1985 BR pocket timetables inadequate and inaccurate, produced its own which were distributed with BR

A souvenir ticket for the first day of opening of the new station at Windermere

Collection. Michael Peascod

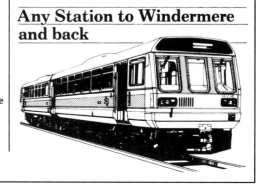

SOUVENIR TICKET

Windermere Station Opening Souvenir Ticket

Thursday 17th April 1986

Any Station to Windermere and back

Valid for one return journey by 'Pacer' train.
Issued in accordance with the Board's Regulations and Conditions.

Ticket No.   ○ ४ ○

approval at stations; some were even taken to Euston. It has also produced information leaflets about the line to help travellers get the most from their visit. By the time of the Action Group's 10th anniversary, traffic on the branch had risen by 40% since its founding.

At the Group's AGM in 1993 there was news of a change to services which saw the reintroduction of through running between Windermere and Manchester, this time to Manchester Airport. This was called, understandably, *the most exciting development since the demise of the 'Club Train'.* The pattern established in May 1994 continues with little change; five trains each day run from Manchester Airport to Windermere. After a return shuttle trip to Oxenholme, they then return via Oxenholme to the airport. This service has been a great success even though it does not start early enough for passengers wanting to catch morning flights. It brings significant numbers of visitors from overseas to the area, as well as giving local users the obvious advantage of a direct service to the centre of Manchester, and is regarded

as one of the jewels in the crown of First North Western, who operate the line. At first these airport trains missed out stops at Burneside and Staveley to save time, though since all the recovery time for the Manchester – Windermere leg was allowed between Kendal and Windermere, these 'expresses' were actually allowed more time for this stretch than the stopping trains! Refinements to the timing now allow Burneside and Staveley to be included as request stops for nearly every train. Burneside Lower crossing, only about 100m from the station, is now a light-controlled open crossing so the train has to slow to 5 mph for this, and therefore stopping at Burneside station adds little time to the journey.

Early and late services are worked as shuttles, so in addition to bringing visitors the line is still used for local journeys to school, work or the shops. In February 1997 the 07.05 Windermere – Oxenholme train was involved in an accident when it ran into the crossing gates at Burneside Higher crossing; for a few weeks trains were

flagged through the crossing until the gates were repaired. The crossing sees much more traffic now than in the past, as Hollins Lane, which crosses the line here, is the preferred route for lorries to Cropper's mill from the main road. There have been regular proposals to convert the Higher crossing to automatic operation, but the date has remained 'in the next financial year'.

Since the revival of the K&W's fortunes in the 1980s it has become increasingly obvious that the line has reached capacity, and though local users, local councils and the train operators would all like to see improved services, the structure of the line makes this impossible. What in the 1970s was seen as reasonable cost cutting is now a constraint. During a two-week closure of the branch in March 2002, full relaying of trackwork was undertaken, together with repairs to major bridges, including the viaduct over the River Kent at Kendal. Hopes have been expressed that the major upgrade of the West Coast Main Line, to carry new, faster and more frequent services operated by Virgin's *Pendolino* and *Voyager* trains, might be followed by works to increase

capacity on the branch. This could include a long running loop at Burneside to allow two trains to pass. However, bearing in mind the disappointments of 1973 and the mid 1980s, one cannot be sure the capacity gain will happen.

It would be unreasonable to end on a negative note. There is much success to recall from the last 20 years. In 1997, for the 150th anniversary of the line's completion, the partnership of Action Group and railway companies came together to celebrate. In 1851 Queen Victoria had sped through Oxenholme on the Royal Train, declining to stop to receive the compliments of Kendal's mayor who was on the platform to greet her. In 1997, thanks to a re-enactment group from Grange-over-Sands, 'Queen Victoria' favoured the K&W by travelling on the celebration train, to be greeted at Windermere by a guard of honour. Speakers and guests at the various ceremonies on 20th April included leading figures from local business, councils and the railway industry, who had all contributed to the day. Councillor Edward Acland from Burneside summed up the feelings of all involved in the celebration with his toast: *Here's to the next 150 years.*

On 20th April 1997 the Action Group and North Western Trains celebrated 150 years of the line. Kevin Brookes of the Oxenholme station staff puts the headboard on the front coach of the 3-car train which took guests from Oxenholme to Windermere.
Photo: Author

Bibliography:

C J Allen: *Titled Trains of Great Britain* (Ian Allan 1953)
Bertram Baxter: *British Locomotive Catalogue 1825-1923* (Moorland Publishing 1978)
Gordon Biddle: *The Railway Surveyors* (Ian Allan 1990)
Harold D Bowtell: *Over Shap to Carlisle* (Ian Allan 1983)
Roger Bingham: *Kendal, a social history* (Cicerone Press)
John Broughton and Nigel Harris: *British Railways Past and Present, Number 1: Cumbria* (Silver Link 1985)
John Alan Cottam: *Elephants on the Line* (Helm Press 1999)
Alexander Frater: *Stopping Train Britain* (Hodder and Stoughton 1983)
John Goodman: *LMS Locomotive Names* (RCTS)
Charles Hadfield and Gordon Biddle: *The Canals of North West England* (David & Charles 1970)
W L Harris and Edward Talbot: *Recollections of Oxenholme* (LNWR Society 1994)
David Jenkinson: *An Illustrated History of LNWR Coaches* (OPC 1978)
David Joy: *Regional History of the Railways of Great Britain, Vol. 14, The Lake Counties* (David & Charles 1983)
Julian Mellentin: *Kendal and Windermere Railway* (Dalesman 1980)
Cornelia Nicholson: *Cornelius Nicholson, a well-spent life* (published 1890)
Railway Gazette: *LMS: Centenary of the Opening of the first Main Line Railway* (Special Supplement 1938)
Brian Reed: *Crewe to Carlisle* (Ian Allan 1969)
M C Reed: *The London and North Western Railway* (Atlantic 1996)
Joe Scott (ed): *A Lakeland Valley through Time* (Staveley and District History Society 1995)
Alex Toye: *Wordsworth's Failure to prevent the Windermere Extension of the LCR* (Unpublished personal study 1997)
Oliver Westall (ed): *Windermere in the 19th Century* (CNWRS, Lancaster 1991)

Appendix 1
Kendal & Windermere Railway Chronology

1837	Publication of 'The London and Glasgow Railway – the Interests of Kendal considered'
Jan 1840	The Longsleddale route presented to the Railway Commissioners
Jul 1840	George Larmer's survey of route via Grayrigg
Apr 1841	The Great North of England Railway opened
Aug 1844	Proposals for the K&WR and Provisional list of Directors published
Oct 1844	Establishment of the Opposition Committee under Prof. Wilson
Nov 1844	Tenders invited for excavation
30 Jun 1845	K&W Act (V8 & 9 c32) An Act for making a railway from the Lancaster & Carlisle Railway to Birthwaite in the Parish of Windermere, to be called 'The Kendal & Windermere Railway'.
16 Jul 1845	Cornelius Nicholson cuts first sod
22 Sep 1846	Opening of line, Kendal – Oxenholme. (the same time as the southern portion of the L&CR)
15 Dec 1846	Formal opening of the L&CR, Oxenholme – Carlisle
17 Dec 1846	Public traffic commenced on L&CR
4 Jan 1847	Start of goods traffic to Kendal
20 Apr 1847	K&WR opened throughout
30 Jun 1848	K&WR Act (11 & 12 Vict. c26) An Act to enable the Kendal & Windermere Railway Company to raise a further sum of money, and to amend the Act relating to such railway
1850	Branch worked under contract by E B Wilson of Leeds
Nov 1851	K&WR assumed control of working the line
Aug 1857	K&W directors agree to the L&C's terms for a lease
1 May 1858	K&W leased in perpetuity by the L&CR
13 Aug 1859	L&CR Act (V22 & 23 c124) An Act for authorising the Lancaster & Carlisle Railway Company to make new works, and to make arrangements with other companies, and to raise further funds; and for other purposes Confirms leasing of K&WR; (both L&C and K&W leased by LNWR)
21 Jul 1879	Dissolution of the K&WR by LNWR
1881	Oxenholme Station rebuilt
1884	Kendal Station enlarged by provision of up platform
1905	The 'Club Train' began running to Manchester
1923	The LNWR became part of the LMS
1924	Cropper's tramway converted to standard gauge
1948	The LMS became part of British Rail's London Midland Region
1962	Oxenholme engine shed closed
1964	Staveley signal box, Staveley and Burneside goods yards closed
1965	Cropper's tramway to Cowan Head closed
1966	The Manchester 'Club Train' ceased running
19 Oct 1967	Staveley level crossing altered to automatic half barriers and crossing box closed
1968	The track layout at Oxenholme was altered, leaving the only access to the Branch by platform 3
28 Apr 1969	Goods facilities withdrawn at Windermere
1971	Burneside and Staveley stations became unstaffed
1972	Final delivery of coal to Cropper's; the final part of the tramway closed
1 May 1972	Goods facilities withdrawn at Kendal
29 Apr 1973	Kendal and Burneside Station signal boxes closed
13 May 1973	The Branch reduced from double to single track; Oxenholme and Windermere signal boxes closed
1980	Announcement of the sale of Windermere station trainshed
Feb 1984	Lakes Line Action Group formed
1986	The new station at Windermere opened
1991	The new shelter opened at Kendal station
May 1994	Through trains to Manchester Airport introduced in the summer timetable
20 Apr 1997	Celebration of 150 years' service on the Branch
Nov 1999	The first stretch of continuous welded rail laid under Reston Bridge
Mar 2002	The Branch closed for 16 days for complete relaying with continuous welded rail.

Appendix 2
Directors of the Kendal & Windermere Railway

BRANDRETH, Lt. Col. Frederick William (1812 – 1883)
Director 1857 - 1859
Residence: Hyning, Milnthorpe   1857 – 1858
              Heaves Lodge, nr Kendal   1859
Married Jane, eldest daughter of James Gandy (1846). He assumed the name of Gandy in lieu of Brandreth in 1859

BRYANS, James
First Director in Act 1845

CLAY, J T
Director 1846

CREWDSON, George Braithwaite
First Director in Act 1845, Director 1846 – 1859
Elected Director August 1846 'in room of J T Clay' who had resigned
Residence   Kendal   1848 – 1855
              Terrace, Windermere   1856 – 1858
              Kendal   1859

CROPPER, James (1823 – 1900)
Director 1847 - 1852
Residence   Cowan Head, nr Kendal   1848 – 1852
Son of James Cropper (1797 – 1874) of Dingle Bank, Liverpool. Bought Burneside and Cowan Head paper mills in 1845
MP for Kendal 1880 - 1885

DAVY, Dr John FRS (1790 – 1868)
Director 1856 - 1859
Residence: Ambleside   1856 – 1859
Friend of Wordsworth and brother of Sir Humphrey Davy, built and lived at Lesketh How, Ambleside

GANDY, James (1787 – 1859)
Director 1848 - 1856
Residence   Heaves Lodge, nr Kendal   1848 – 1856

GANDY, John
First Director in Act 1845, Director *1845* – 1856
Chairman *1848* – 1854
Residence   Kendal   1848 –1852
              Elleray, Windermere   1853 – 1855
              Oaklands, Windermere   1856

HARRISON, Edmund (1802 – 1870)
Director 1853 - 1859
Residence   Old Hall, Westmorland   1853 – 1854
              Abbot Hall   1855 – 1859
Twin brother of John Harrison

HARRISON, John (1802 - 1884)
Director 1847 - 1852
Residence   Hundhowe, nr Kendal   1848 – 1852
Twin brother of Edmund Harrison

HEYWORTH, Lawrence (1786 - 1872)
Director 1853 – 1859
Chairman 1855 – 1859
Residence   Liverpool   1853 – 1856
              Yew Tree Lodge, Liverpool   1856 - 1859
MP for Derby 1848 - 1857

NICHOLSON, Cornelius
First Director in Act 1845

PARKER, Francis
Director 1857 - 1859
Residence   Sydenham   1857 – 1859

ROBERTS, Thomas
Director 1848 - 1851
Residence   Manchester   1848 – 1851

WANKLYN, T B Director *1846 - 1847*

WHITWELL, John (1811 – 1880)
Director 1845 – 1859
Deputy Chairman 1855 - 1859
Residence   Kendal   1848 – 1859
Of Bank House, Kendal, carpet manufacturer, built the wool warehouse on Beezon Field, served by its own rail line which crossed the road
Mayor of Kendal 1854, 1856, 1862, 1863, 1865 & 1867
MP for Kendal 1868 – 1880
President of the Association of Chambers of Commerce of the United Kingdom, 1880

WHITWELL, William (1809 – 1890)
First Director in Act 1845, Director *1845* - 1852
Residence   Towerson Hall, nr Kendal   1848 –1852

WILSON, Edward (1796 – 1870)
Mentioned in Act 1845
Residence   Abbott Hall
Banker, grandson of Christopher Wilson, a founder, in 1788, of Maude, Wilson and Crewdson's Bank, Kendal
High Sheriff of Westmorland 1851

WILSON, John Hewetson
First Director in Act 1845

WILSON, John Jowitt (1809 – 1875)
First Director in Act 1845
Director *1848* – 1854
Deputy Chairman *1848* – 1854
Residence   Kendal   1848 – 1854
              Of Kent Terrace, Kendal
Mayor of Kendal 1853 & 1857

Note: Dates in *italic* are not confirmed.

Back Cover:
The illustration of Windermere Station in LNWR days is from a coloured post card from the collection of Richard D Foster. The ornate drinking fountain has been moved to the Brewery Arts Centre in Kendal.

Train on the road! Cropper's Ruston diesel engines goes through Burneside on the tramway to Bowston and Cowan Head. Photo: Margaret Duff Collection.

The series of contemporary LNWR tickets are from the collection of Glynn Waite, and are reproduced his kind permission.